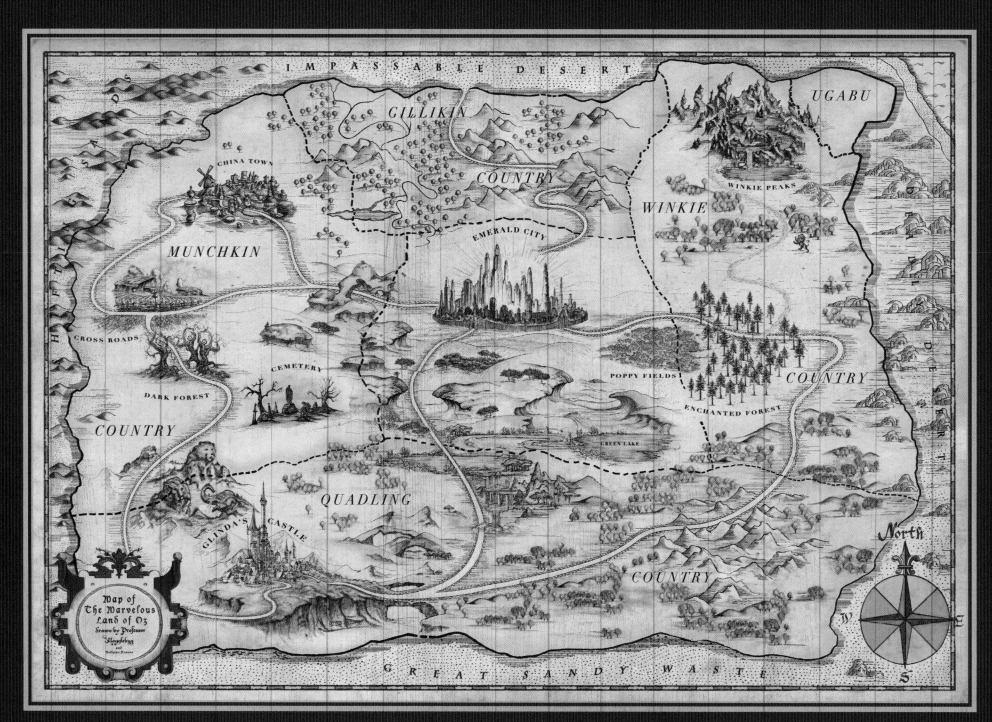

LAND OF OZ MAP used for the film. Artwork by Andrea Dopaso.

THE ART OF Oz

Disney

THE GREAT AND POWERFUL

BY GRANT CURTIS

WITH PHOTOGRAPHS BY MERIE WALLACE

Published by Disney Editions, an imprint of Disney Book Group. No part of this
book may be reproduced or transmitted in any form or by any means, electronic
or mechanical, including photocopying, recording, or by any information storage
and retrieval system, without written permission from the publisher.

For more information address Disney Editions,
114 Fifth Avenue, New York, New York 10011

Editors: Michael Siglain and Nachie Castro
Designed by: OFFSETS

The makers of this book would like to thank Brittany Candau, Jennifer Eastwood,
Warren Meislin, Scott Piehl, Rich Thomas, Marybeth Tregarthen, Jason
Wojtowicz, Lauren Yenokida, Jennifer Curtis, Dan Curtis, Linda Curtis,
Jeremy Wheeler, Sam Raimi, Joe Roth, Palak Patel, Josh Donen,
Philip Steuer, Robert Stromberg, Ernie Malik, and Merie Wallace.

Extra special thanks to research assistant Nellie Prestine-Lowery
and contributing writer Elizabeth Rudnick.

ISBN 978-1-4231-7091-4
F322-8368-0-13060
Printed in the United States of America
First Edition
10 9 8 7 6 5 4 3 2 1

Visit www.disneybooks.com and www.disney.com/thewizard.

D23
The Official Disney Fan Club
Disney.com/D23

SUSTAINABLE FORESTRY INITIATIVE
Certified Chain of Custody
At Least 30% Certified Forest Content
www.sfiprogram.org
SFI-01429

FOR TEXT PAPER ONLY

OZ LANDSCAPE LION STUDY by Dylan Cole.

OZ'S BALLOON approaches a Kansas storm.
Illustration by Dylan Cole.

INTRODUCTION

THIS IS THE SECOND TIME I HAVE BEEN BLESSED by the opportunity to record the creative and technical endeavors that transpired in order to bring a major motion picture to the silver screen; my first book was *The Spider-Man Chronicles: The Art and Making of Spider-Man 3*.

In both instances, the sense of honor I have felt as I have been able to present the art of others, the photographs of others, and the various labors of love of others has been immense, while the regrets have been few and quite specific. Namely, there is one: the simple fact that there are so many key contributions, key names, that inevitably are absent from the pages you are about to read. It is impossible to journal everything and everyone, and unsurprisingly that is the disappointment that lingers.

There are certain names repeated often in the chapters ahead, while others are hardly mentioned, or not mentioned at all even though their contributions deserved their own chapter. Names such as: Josh Donen, Philip Steuer, Mark McNair, Matt Hirsch, Brittney Nance, Tom Udell, K.C. Hodenfield, Peter Deming, John Papsidera, Rick Firkins, Lesley Kay, Jeff Passanante, Bob Murawksi, Michael LaViolette, Phil Sloan, Yolanda Toussieng, Vivian Baker, Nana Fischer, Russell Bobbitt, Ernie Malik, Becky Boyle, Nancy Haigh, Petur Hliddal, Tamara Watts Kent, John Frazier, Jim Schwalm, David Lowery, Marc Vena, Jeff Henderson, Phillip Keller, Oliver Thomas, Jeremy Thompson, Scott Rogers, Randy Beckman, Barry Howell, Trevor Tuttle, Geno Hart, Ian Kelly, Michael Herron, Ed Marsh, Jeffrey Lynch, Jeff Okabayashi, Paul Sanchez, Danny Elfman, Jussi Tegelman, Marti Humphrey, Chris Jacobson, Lance Burton, Jody Fedele, Susan Dudeck, and Debbi Bossi—just to name a few. Additionally, there is a facility and city briefly mentioned in the following odyssey that deserves a special mention. *Oz The Great and Powerful* was the first film to shoot at the world-class Michigan Motion Picture Studios in Pontiac, Michigan, and the hospitality we encountered there and in the surrounding cities made our time away from our own homes a special experience.

In an effort to recognize the incredible contribution of everyone who worked on *Oz The Great and Powerful*, I have listed the names of our entire cast and crew as of the moment this book was pried from my fingers. There will be some people in postproduction that have yet to be hired that do not appear. To those individuals I apologize for the unavoidable, and I dedicate the pages within to our entire cast and crew. Thank you for an unforgettable journey down the Yellow Brick Road.

OUTSIDE THE EMERALD CITY GATES
by Robert Stromberg and Dylan Cole.

RUBEN ABARCA • BILL ABBOTT • CRAIG ABELE • PHILLIP ABEYTA • KATE ABRAHAM • GARY ABRAHAMIAN • SEM ABRAHAMS • JONATHEN ABRAMS • LILIA ACEVEDO • JAMES ACHATZ • ADAM COGGIN • MARK ADLER • MERAV ADLER • ARNOLD AGEE • CRYSTAL AGUILAR • ROBERT AGUILAR • HARRY AKERS • JAMES AKERS • TALIA AKIVA • ZADE AKKAD • KEREN ALBALA • STEVEN ALESSI • BROOKLYN ALEXANDER • MUKTSAR ALI • JOSEPH ALLEGRO • BERNARD ALLEMON • BERNIE ALLEMON • DONAVAN ALLEN • GEORGIA ALLEN • ALEXANDER ALLEN • CHYNA ALLEN • ROBERT ALLEN • ANTONIO ALMARAZ • RICHARD ALONZO • ISA ALSUP • RACHEL ALTERMAN • SALVATORE ALUIA • STEVE ALVARADO • LUIS ALVAREZ • OZZY ALVAREZ • ANDREW AMATO • ANDREA AMATO • RYAN AMBORN • CLAUDIA AMBRIZ • WILLIAM AMBROSE • SALVADOR ANAYA • KIMBER ANDERSON • MICHAEL ANDERSON • STEVEN ANDERSON • KAREN ANDERSON • ROBERT ANDERSON • AMY ANDREWS • HOLLIS ANDREWS • TRACY ANDREWS • JEFF ANDRUS • CRAIG ANDUJAR • JOSEPH ANTHONY • VARSENIK ANTONYAN • LILIK ANTONYAN • MILAIN ANTOUN • CAROL APCZYNSKI • JASON APPERSON • MARK ARANDA • FRED ARBEGAST • STEPHANIE ARBLE • ANNEMARIE ARCURI • MICHAEL ARDELEAN • LYNDA ARNOLD • NICK ARNOLD • KAITLYN ARNOLD • MICHAEL AROLA • JON ARTURI • DEBORAH ASH • TIFFANY ASKEW • DAVID ATHERTON • HUNTER ATHEY • MARVIN ATLAS • FAHIMA ATROUNI • ROSS ATTARD • LATOYA ATTERBERRY • GREGG ATWELL • ADRIA AUGUST • JANE AULL • ADAM AUSTIN • BENNETT AUSTIN • MARK AUSTIN • MARYELLEN AVIANO • EDWARD AVILA • ISIDORO AVILA • AMBER AXELTON • ERIN AYALP • JUSTIN AYERS • ROBERT AYERS • RON AYERS • H.B. AARIS • RYAN BABBS • MICHAEL BABCOCK • JENNIFER BABIAN • JONATHAN BACH • DONALD BACON • DEREK BACON • KELLY BACON • APOLLO BACULA • BLAISE BADALAMENT • CHESTER BADALATO • GILBERT BADILLO • SHANNON BAKEMAN • CARLOS BAKER • DANA BAKER • JAMES BAKER • SCOTT BAKER • BARBARA BAKER • DENISE BAKER • EDWIN BAKER • VIVIAN BAKER • GREGORY BALLARD • SCOTT BALLEW • DAWN BALLOU • MARK BALLOU • ARCHIE BANE • JOSEPH BANE • CHRISTOPHER BANGMA • KELLEY BANKS • BILL BANYAI • TODD BARANOWSKI • RON BARATONO • JOHN BARBER • F.LE BARDHA • WESLEY BARKER • BEN BARKER • ROBERT BARNES JR. • CAMERON BARNETT • DAVID BARNUM • THOMAS BARONE

ALYSSA BARR • EARL BARR • TIM BARRETT • SEAN BARRY • BRANDY BARTNICK • YURI BARTOLI • RENZO BARTOLOTTA • KENNETH BARTOS • MICHAEL BARUZZINI • NEIL BASTIAN • JOSEPH BATES • CHRISTIAN BATTISTE • TASHA BATTLE • MATT BAUER • THOMAS BAUER • HUNTER BAUM • MIKE BAUMAN • DANIEL BAXTER • JEFF BAYER • ANDREW BAYS • BENJAMIN BAZMORE • BERT BEATSON • ROBIN BEAUCHESNE • KAREN BECK • BRANDON BECKMAN • RANDY BECKMAN • SHELLI BECKMAN • DONALD BECKS • SABRINA BEDRANI • CHARLES BEESLEY • FRANKLIN BEESLEY JR. • JOHN BELANGER • JOSEPH BELCZAK • RICHARD BELL • CORBIN BELL • ROBERT BELL • ERIN BELLER • MICHAEL BELT • NELSON BELTRAN • TERRIEN BEN • JOHN BENETTI • DONALD BENNETT • JOHN BENTLEY • TROY BENTON • HOWARD BERGER • DEREK BERK • MICHAEL BERLUCCHI • CRAIG BERNATZKE • CLIFF BERNS • CHARLENE BERRY • DANIEL BESOCKE • STACY BEVERLY • EDWARD BEY • KEVIN BEY • SARENA BHARGAVA • MELISSA BICKERTON • JEANNE BIJKERK-PIPPIN • MICHAEL BINCZEK • JOSEPH BINGENHEIMER • FRANK BIONDO • JAMES BIRD • DONALD BISHOP • MATT BISHOP • ROBERT BISSONNETTE • CHARLY BIVONA • JOURDAN BIZIOU • MICHAEL BJERKE • PAMELA BLACK • RYDER BLACKBURN • CHRISTINE BLACKER • CARL BLAIR • KENLEY BLAKE • KYMBER BLAKE • WALTER BLAKE KNOBLOCK • HORACIO BLANCO • CHRISTOPHER BLASKO • KEVIN BLAUVELT • STEPHEN BLOCH • RON BLOCH • ANDREW BLUMSACK • JORDAN BOBBITT • RUSSELL BOBBITT • RICK BOBIER • WILLIAM BOCK • DAVID BOHORQUEZ • ROBERT BOLDT • MARK BOLEY • DAVID BOLLMAN • ALICJA BOLTRYK • AUSTIN BONANG • CYNTHIA BOND • BROOKE BOND • ROOSEVELT BONNER • JOHN BONNIN • THOMAS BOOKOUT • BRYAN BOOTH • JOHN LORD BOOTH III • SHUNIL BORPUJARI • DEBBI BOSSI • BOYD BOSSLER • MICHAEL BOU-MAROUN • MIKAYLA BOUCHARD • MARK BOUCHER • ANTHONY BOURA • FRANK BOURNE • JAKE BOWEN • TOM BOWEN • JEROME BOWIE • MARVIN BOWIE • CHAD BOWMAN • DEREK BOWMAN • MARK BOYCE • ROGER BOYD II • MARK BOYER • BECKY BOYLE • BRIAN BOYNTON • CHRISTOPHER BRACKEN • JACOB BRADES • JOHN BRADLEY • ZACH BRAFF • CYNTHIA BRAGA • ERIC BRAKKE • CHARLES BRAMER • ROCKIE BRANDENBURG

MICHIGAN MOTION PICTURE STUDIOS, where *Oz The Great and Powerful* was filmed.

• Eleyna Brandt • Michelle Brattson •
Keith Braun • Jose Bravo • David Brayman •
John Breedlove • Brian Breithaupt • Robert
Brenner • Georgiana Brent • Jack Bresewitz
• Matthew Brewer • Carter Briggs •
Jaqueline Briggs • Wayne Brinston • Chris
Brock • Geoffrey Brock • Erika Broderdorf
• Timothy Broderick • Richard Brondum •
Jeffrey Brooks • Jerrold Brooks • Kim
Brooks • Ashley Broome • Robert Broski •
Brian Brown • Elizabeth Brown • Thomas
Brown • Abigail Brown • Austin Brown •
Christopher Brown • Jacqueline Brown •
Joshua Brown • William Brown • Tanya
Brown Walker • Arnie Bruinsma • Jason
Brunelle • Tuan Bruno Nguyen • Jack

Chacon • Grady Chambless • Alexander
Chance • William Chapman • G. Charlie
Brewer • Douglas Chartier • Mike Chavez
• Maria Chavez • Corey Checketts • Peggy
Chen • Albert Cheng • Andy Cheng • Rena
Cheng • Todd Cherniawsky • Jonathan
Cherup • Mike Chiado • Catherine Childers
• Joseph Childs • Judy Chin • Robert
Chinello • Clifton Chippewa II • Chul Cho
• Ashlynn Chong • Jones Chris • Michael
Christian • Tony Chromie • Justin

Brusewitz • J. Bryan Holloway • Chris Bryant • Gregory Bryant • Thomas Bryant •
Annemarie Bryant • Derlin Brynford-Jones • Todd Buchanan • Robert Buck • Donna
Buckley • Gary Buckner • Rachel Buechele • Andre Bufalini • Jim Buford • Steve Bui
• Matthew Bulleri • Pierre Bunikiewicz • Zachary Bunker • Steven Bunyea • Jonathan
Burdeshaw • Jordan Burgess • George Burket • Brad Burkhardt • John Burnette •
Tiffany Burns • Tom Burns • Van Burns • Alaric Burton • Christy Busby • John
Bustamante • Chelsea Butterfield • Alexander Byrum • Tony Cabrera • Lorren
Cackoski • Kevin Cadwallader • Kevin Caffrey • Gregory Callaghan • Greg Callas
• William Calvert • Jennifer Calzacorto • Michael Camerella • Michael Camilleri •
Burton Campbell • John Campbell • Keith Campbell • Todd Campbell • William
Campbell • Bruce Campbell • Don Campbell • Josh Campbell • Francisco Campos •
Geovani Campos • John Canavan • Eyan Candini • Thomas Cannon • Haskell Canter IV
• Jennifer Caprio • Andrea Carlson • Ariel Carlson • Nathaniel Carlson • Michael
Carmody • Bruce Carothers • Timothy Carr • Cristen Carr Strubbe • Gail Carroll-
Coe • David Carter • Paul Carter • Sean Carter • Fashon Carter • Roderick Carter
• Frank Casaceli III • Joe Casares • Christopher Casey • John Casey • Matthew Casey
• Michael Casey • Shoghi Castel De Oro • Liliam Castellena • Laurence Castello •
David Castillo • Anna Catherine Burd Kelly • Steve Catherman • Thomas Caton • Ron
Causey • Johnny Cayton • Jesse Cecchini • Larry Cedar • Thomas Centers • Ruben

Chrzanowski • Dino Cinciarelli • Rodney Cinkan • Suzanne Cipolletti • Kenneth
Ciszewski • Steve Clack • Alfred Claramunt • Jeremy Clark • Will Clarke • Tye
Claybrook • Tyrone Claybrooke • Stacy Clinger • Michael Clossin • Daniel Clouser
• Sean Clouser • Aferdita Clouser • Sarah Coatts • Bill Cobbs • Joseph Cobos • Emilie
Cockels • Matthew Codd • Ronald Coden • Dave Coffey • David Cohen • Cody
Cohoon • Jeffrey Cole • Dylan Cole • Daniel Collick • Mia Collie • Richard Collins
• Jamee Collins • Timothy Collins • Kyle Colton • Marlene Comanescu • Jimmy Combs
• Mark Connelly • Michael Conner • Kit Conners • Michael Connor • Arthur
Contreras Jr. • Jeremy Cook • Jeremiah Cooke • William Cooley • Frederick Cooper •
Jesse Cooper • Kenneth Cooper • Gillian Cooper • Thomas Cooper • Wallace Corbeill
• James Corley • Brandon Cornell • Brooks Cornell • Thomas Cornell • Catherine
Cornell • Darrell Corr • Gary Corr Jr. • William Corso • Elizabeth Cortez • Ross
Coscia • Anne Costa • Dan Cota • Warren Cotner • Sharon Courtney • Ja'vonne
Cousins • Chris Couto • Darryl Cowherd Jr. • Joe Cox • Alphonso Cox • David
Crabtree • Zachary Craft • Justin Cragin • Jennifer Cram • Travis Craven • Brian
Crawford • Duncan Crawford • Clark Credle • Jane Crile • Rob Crites • Sean
Crockatt • Betty Croft • Gino Crognale • Richard Crompton • Laurence Cropley •
Joseph Croskey • Donn Cross • Natalie Cross • Joseph Crouch • Amber Crowe • Kim
Cruchon-Brooks • April Crump • Dorothy Crutcher • Ian Cummings • Brandon

CUNDIFF • ZAC CUNNINGHAM • LAURI CUPPETILLI • NICK CURDY • GRANT CURTIS • MICHELE CUSICK • ADAM CUTHBERT • WENDY CUTLER • JOE CUZAN • KEOMANY CYNOWA • BRITT CYRUS • VINCENT D'AQUINO • ANDREW D'ASCENZO • EMMET DACEY • MATTHEW DACO • JOSH DAGG • THOMAS DAGUANNO • JOHN DAILY • MICHAEL DAILY • MATTHEW DAKHO • MATTHEW DAKHO • DIAN DAKROUB • LAIAL DAKROUB • JEFFREY DALDIN • CHRIS DAME • CHARLES DAMRON • T. DANIEL SCARINGI • CHRISTOPHER DANIELS • DEBBIE DARAKDJIAN • ADRIANA DARDAS • GARY DARE • MICHAEL DAULT • DON DAVIDOSKI • ALMA DAVILA-TORO • JAMES DAVIS • STACY DAVIS • DERMOT DAVIS • EUGENE DAVIS • TRACEY DAVIS • JAIME DAWKINS • KALEN DAWSON • SALVADOR DE ANDA • ROSEMARY DE CICCO • GABRIEL DE CUNTO • JAMES DE GEETER • ROMMYN DE LEEUW • ANGEL DE SANTI • SAMUEL DEAN • ZACHARY DEATER • JERRY DEATS • SARAH DEBOER • STEVE DECASTRO • TOM DECEMBER • STEFAN DECHANT • ROBERT DECOURT • TROY DEDERICK • DEE DEE ALLEMON • SARAH DEFORD • KIM DEGRAAF • RON DEGUZMAN • IDEENE DEHDASHTI • COREY DEIST • STEVAN DEL GEORGE • COCO DEL SIGNORE • RYDER DEL SIGNORE • CONSTANCE DELCOURT • ED DELOMPREY • SARAH DELUCCHI • JOSEPH DEMARSH • DENNIS DEMBECK • KATE DEMING • PETER DEMING • JOHN DEMONACO • CEDRIC DEMPS • CHUCK DEMSKE • THEODORE DEMSKI • NICOLE DEMSKI • ETHAN DENK • BRIAN DENNIS • ROBERT DEPEW • ERIC DEREN • JOHN DESZI • SCOTT DEVIER • LESLIE DEVLIN • JAMES DEVLIN • JACOB DEWITT • JOHN DEZSI • CAROLE DHUMPHREYS • KENNETH DIAZ • SUZANNE DIAZ • ROBERT DIAZ • WILLIAM DICENSO • WILLIAM DICK • TONY DICKENS • ARTURO DICKEY • GRETCHEN DICKINSON • JAMES DICKSON • GERALD DIETE-SPIFF • SHIRLEEN DIFONZO • JOHN DILLON • DAVID DILSIZIAN • MICHAEL DINGESS • JAKE DINNAN • OMAR DIOP • TRACY DIXON • DANIEL DOBBS • RYAN DODDS • DOUGLAS DOLE • CLARISSA DOMINGUEZ • EMILY DOMINGUEZ • ERICK DONALDSON • JOSHUA DONEN • RONALD DOOLEY • ROY DOOLEY JR. • ANDREA DOPASO • JAMES DORDA • ROXANNE DORMAN • CHRISTOPHER DOROWSKY • ANDREW DOROWSKY • JOHN DORRIEN • SABRINA DORRIEN • ANDREW DOUCETTE • SCOTT DOUGHERTY • JOSHUA DOVE • FRED DOVE JR. • DANIELLA DOYEN • LISA DOYLE • NIK DRAGICEVIC • VAL DRAKE • LENA DRAKE • BILL DRAPER • BRAD DRAPER • MICHELLE DRAPINSKI • DALE DREW

GREGORY DREWNO • MARK DRUM • DAVID DRZEWIECKI • RACHEL DUBAY • DONALD DUBORD • DEREK DUBYAK • ALCIE DUCKETT • SUSAN DUDECK • MATTHEW DUDLEY • KENNETH DUDLEY • ANTONY DUGANDZIC • DONTEL DUHART • DAVID DUNBAR • ALEXANDER DUNN • DAVID DUPUIS • STEPHAN DUPUIS • LEANTE DUREN • JOHN DUTCHER • JUSTIN DYBOWSKI • ABRAHAM DYCK • TED EACHUS • SCOTT EAGLE • BRUCE EALY • PHAEDRA EASON • TIM EASTERDAY • JOHN EAVES • KEN EBERT • CHRISTOPHER ECKLES • ELISE EDSON • LARRY EDWARDS • ALONZO EDWARDS • CHASE EDWARDS • CHRISTY EDWARDS • GUY EDWARDS • KEVIN EDWARDS • SUMMER EDWARDS • TIFFANI EDWARDS • JOE EKPENE • JESSE EKPENE II • PHIL ELAM • DANNY ELFMAN • MICHELLE ELIAS • THEO ELIAS • JOSH ELLEDGE • COLE ELLER • BRAD ELLIOTT • DODSON ELLIOTT • ROYDEN ELLIOTT • ISAAC ELLIS • PATRICK ELLIS • JOHNNY ELLSWORTH • JOSEPH ELROM • JASON ENDRES • LEONARD ENGELMAN • CHRISTOPHER ENGLE • DAN ENGLE • JOHN ENGLISH • COURTNEY ENGLISH • GEOFFREY ERNST • CONSTANCE ESPOSITO • MIKE ESTES • BRADLEY ETHERIDGE • JULIE ETHERIDGE • DAVID EUBANK • JAMES EVANS • LAUREN EWANICK • MELISSA EXELBERTH • JACKSON EZINGA • NINA FABIO • LIAM FAIRBANKS • JUSTIN FALGOUT • MITCHELL FALK • KEVIN FANNON • MARY-JANE FARIS • NIGEL FAULKNER • RYAN FAULKNER • DAVID FAVENYESI • MOLLY FAYE • CORMICK FEARON • JON FEDELE • JODY FEDELE • MONICA FEDRICK • ANDREW FEKETE • EVAN FEKETE • KATHY FENNESSY • KEELY FERGUSON • DAVID FERNANDEZ • ELOY FERNANDEZ • GREGORY FERNANDEZ • JOHN FERREIRA • JACKSON FERRELL • EVAN FEUERMAN • JOSHUA FICKEN • PATRICK FIELD • JOHN FIELDING • BRAD FILLMANN • JORDAN FIMEGAN • ENRICO FIN • STEVE FINLEY • MATT FINNEMORE • NICHOLAS FIRKINS • RICHARD FIRKINS • NANA FISCHER • NAOKO FISCHER • ALISON FISHER • MADISON FISHER • STEFANI FLACK • JOHN FLAHERTY • PATRICK FLANAGAN • DALE FLANIGAN • MICHAEL FLAVIN • JAMES FLEMMING • OSCAR FLORES • MICHAEL FLORIDA • ROBERT FLOYD • HEATHER FLYNN • MICHAEL FLYNN • TRAVIS

(CLOCKWISE FROM BOTTOM RIGHT) Hair Dept. Head Yolanda Toussieng, Co-Key Hair Stylist Jules Holdren, Ms. Kunis' Makeup Artist Tracey Levy, Mr. Franco's Hair/Makeup Artist Nana Fischer, and cast liaison Ray Gordon II. Photograph by Merie Wallace.

FLYNN • CHRISTINA FONG • MARK FORBES • STEVE FORBES • CHARLES FORD • JACQUELYN FOREMAN • MELISSA FORNEY • TODD FORSBERG • MARY ANN FORSTER • CIARRA FORSYTH • TIMOTHY FORT • STEPHEN FOSS • BEAU FOSTER • ELIZABETH FOSTER • NICHOLAS FOSTER • DOUGLAS FOX • MARY FOX • CARLY FRANCAVILLA • EVONNE FRANCESCHINI • TOM FRANCHETT • ANTONIO FRANCHI • JAMES FRANCO • MELISSA FRANCO • ELIZABETH FRANK • ALEX FRANK • MARCUS FRANKEL • CHRIS FRANKOVICH • ANTHONY FRATTINI • ERIC FRAZIER • JOHN FRAZIER • MARSHALL FRAZIER • STEPHEN FREEBAIRN • JOSH FREIHEIT • EDWARD FRENCH • DAVID FRENCH • LISA FRESARD • CHAD FREY • KENNY FREZZELL • DONNALYNN FRIEDMAN •

1ST ASSISTANT DIRECTOR K.C. HODENFIELD.
Photograph by Merie Wallace.

GOODWIN • EDWARD GORDON • RHONA GORDON • RAY GORDON II • EDWARD GOREE • JULIA GORIAL • CONNOR GORMAN • KIMBERLY GOWRIE • SEAN GOWRIE • JAMES GRABER • MIKE GRABOWSKI • MARC GRACE • MICHAEL GRADY • DEREK GRAF • ALEX GRAFF • MICHAEL GRAHAM • JACKI GRAHAM • ANDREA GRANADOS • CLAYTON GRANGER • JEFFREY GRANT • ROD GRANT • SCOTT GRANT • BRANDON GRANTZ • SUZANNE GRASSO • CARL GRATKOWSKI • JOHN GRAY • RYAN GRAY ANDERSON • MICHELE GRAYBEAL • RENEE GREATHOUSE • MARK

JOSHUA FRIZ • NICK FROLLO • JEFFREY FROST • SPENCER FROST • COREY FROWNFELTER • LOGAN FRY • JEFF FUJITA • TREVOR FULKS • GREGORY FULLER • DAMIAN FULLER • GREGORY FUNK • ROLLIE GACKSTETTER • ALEXANDER GAETA • CHRISTOPHER GALLAHER • JANE GALLI • SANDRA GALLO-HARRISON • GODOFREDO GANNOD • KATIE GARAGIOLA-EARLEY • TONI GARAVAGLIA • ANTHONY GARCIA • ESTEBAN GARCIA • NICHOLAS GARCIA • DAVID GARDNER • KEN GARDNER • NEAL GARON • KENNETH GARRETT • LYNN GARRIDO • MADISON GARTNER • GARY GARZA • RUBEN GARZA • STUART GATES • ALINA GATTI • STEVE GAUB • ERIC GAVLINSKI • ROBYN GEBHART • GARY GEDDRY • DANIEL GEER • KURT GEFKE • RYAN GENTHER • JOE GEORGE • PATRICK GEORGE • ELIZABETH GEORGOFF • JOHN GERASIMSO • ERIC GERKE • DENNIS GERMAIN • JULIE GERSHENSON • JUSTIN GERSTENBERGER • SUSAN GERTNER • AHMED GHANI • LORA GIANINO • MICHAEL GIANNINI • MARTIN GIBBONS • PENNY GIBBS • JOSH GIBERT • CARLA GIBSON • CURBY GIBSON • JANE GIBSON • DANIEL GILBERT • JACOB GILBERT • NICKOLAS GILBERT • CAMRYN GILLENWATER • DANIEL GILLESPIE • CATHERINE GILLESPIE • MEGAN GILLIAM • DERRICK GILLIAM • JOE GILLIGAN • DANIEL GILLOOLY • BRITTANY GILPIN • SEAN GINEVAN • LUKE GINGRAS • KEN GIPSON • DANUT GIRNET • ROY GITTENS JR • ELIJAH GIVEN • KAITLIN GLADEN • CHRISTOPHER GLASS • JOHN GLENN JR. • MARK GODDU • JAKE GODZAK • CHRISTOPHER GOE • BRYAN GOETZINGER • CARMINE GOGLIA • JAMES GOLDMAN • DAVID GOLDMAN • TIM GOMES • FRANCISCO GOMEZ • JERARDO GOMEZ • JOE GONZALES • RICHARD GONZALES • ALICIA GONZALEZ • SAUL GONZALEZ • LINDSAY GOOD • DAVID GOODMAN • TOMMY

GREEN • JOHN GREEN • RENE GREEN • STEPHEN GREENBERG • ROBERT GREENFIELD III • JOSHUA GREER • KELLY GREGSON • JAMES GRESSNER • STEPHEN GREY • JOSHUA GRIDLEY • ANTHONY GRIFFIN • DALLAS GRIFFIN • ROXANE GRIFFIN • SHANE GRIFFIN • TAD GRIFFITH • TODD GRIFFITH • ALEXANDER GRIFFITHS • LEE GRIMES • ERIK GRIOTT • CHARLES GRISHAM • RANDY GRIZZLE • DAN GRUENWALD • ROBERT GUALDONI • CHRIS GUARDIOLA • CRAIG GUBERT • JOHN GUCIARDO • ANTHONY GUERRERO • ASLEY GUERRERO • KACIE GUGGIA • KRISTA GUGGIA • CHESTER GUILMET • LEE GULU • BRIGITA GUMSEY • JEFFREY GUNNELLS • MICHAEL GUTHRIE • SCOTT GUTHRIE • RENE GUY • VIVIAN GUZMAN • JOE GUZMAN • CAITLIN GWINN • ANH HA • JOSHUA HACKNEY • TAMYRA HACKNEY • CHRISTOPHER HAGAN • ANDREW HAGEN • BRIAN HAGERTY • NANCY HAIGH • JOHN HAINES • NEDRA HAINEY • ELISE HALBERT • ALEXA HALE • KEVIN HALL • MARY HALL • ROBERT HALL • CHRISTOPHER HAMBLIN • STEVEN HAMILTON • BRANDON HAMILTON • LUMAS HAMILTON • GRANTHAM HAMM • MARC HAMMER • OLIVIA HANDLEY • KEVIN HANEY • ELIE HANG • VICTOR HANG • SCOTT HANKEL • SHANE ACKER • STEVEN HANNA • CHERIE HAPPY • KIRT HARDING • DIANNE HARDY • JASON HARMER • ALLISON HARREY • JESSE HARRINGTON • CHRISTOPHER HARRINGTON • DAVID HARRIS • KEMPER HARRIS • MARY HARRIS • RICK HARRIS • SAM HARRISON • JIMMY HARRITOS • GENO HART • STEPHEN HART • PAUL HART • IAN HARTSHORN • DON HASTINGS • FELECIA HATCHER-BROWN • LARRY HATHORNE • NATHAN HATTON • JUSTIN HAUT • CHARLIE HAVILAND • JEFFREY HAWKINS • MATTHEW HAWKINS • URSULA HAWKS • ROBBIN HAWTHORNE • LARRY HAWTHORNE • KAREN

COMPOSER DANNY ELFMAN.
Photograph by Merie Wallace.

KLAU • ELAINE KLAUS • MARTIN KLEBBA • JONATHAN KLEIN • DENNIS KLEINSMITH • JULIUS KLINE • TOMMY KLINES • HILARY KLYM • BRIAN KMETZ • CHRISTOPHER KMETZ • GEOFFREY KNIGHT • STEVE KNOLL • BRADLEY KNOPF • DANIEL KNOWLTON • JOHN KNOWLTON • JOHNATHAN KNOWLTON • JONAS KNOWLTON • LEROY KNUDSEN • AMANDA KOCEFAS • ALLISON KOCHANSKI • KATHLEEN KOCHISH • CALLIE KOENING • BRANDON KOEPSELL • ADAM KOGELMAN • KATE KOGELMAN • CALEB KOILPILLA • KATHLEEN KOLACZ • DOUG KOLBICZ • TOM KOLLENBERG • DIANE KONDEK • KENNY KONDRATKO • ANNA KOORIS • LAURA KOPYTEK • GREGORY KORDEK • JERREMY KORONA • DAVID KORPALSKI • ALEXANDER KOSTAN • KEVIN

DIRECTOR OF PHOTOGRAPHY PETER DEMING.
Photograph by Merie Wallace.

• ROSEMARY LIMES-ZEIGER • DAVID LINDSAY-ABAIRE • NICHOLAS LINDSAY-ABAIRE • LOUIS LINDWALL • THOMAS LINIARSKI II • FELICIA LINSKY • EDWARD LINSLEY • LINDA LINSLEY • TIM LINSLEY • BRANDON LINVILLE • ERIC LIPSKY • CARL LIPSON • JOSEPH LISANTI • RALPH LISTER • ELIE LITTAUER • BRANDON LIU • IRENE LIU • ROGER LIU • SAM LIU • VERONICA LIU • RICH LIVERANCE • NOAH LOBO • KATHRYN LOCH • JOSE LOFTIN • MATTHEW LOMBARDO • HOWARD LONDON • LINDA LONG • SAMUEL LONG • BRADLEY LOOK • EDWIN LOOL • RAFAEL LOPEZ

KOTLAR • BRANDON KOVATCH • KEN KOWALSKI • DAVID KRAMER • FRANCIS KRANZ • ALAINA KRAUS • ELYSE KRAUSMANN • EDWARD KRISOR • EMILY KROPP • WAYNE KROSCH • KYLE KRYSTYAN • STEVEN KUCHARSKI • RONALD KUDZIA • SANDRA KUE • CHRISTOPHER KUHL • RICHARD KUHN • CHELSEA KULBACK • MILA KUNIS • RYAN KUNKLEMAN • TOM KURSZEWSKI • ROBERT KURTZMAN • LARRY KUSEK • MICHAEL KUTSCHE • CURT KUTSCHER • MARTIN KUTYLO • ANDREW KUZNER • STEVE LA PORTE • JAMES LACEY • JESSICA LACH • MIKE LADACH • FRANK LAFATA • PAUL LAFOND • TRAVIS LAGUIRE-QUINN • NANCY LAI • COLLIN LALONDE • MAX LALONDE • RICHARD LAMB • TOBY LAMM • RICHARD LAMPHIEAR • ELLEN LAMPL • MICHAEL LANDAUER • RAYMOND LANDINO JR. • MARK LANDON • PETER LANDRY • BETTY LANE • JESSICA LANE • RANDY LANGFORD • HEATHER LANGMEYER • DWAYNE LANGS • RUBEN LANGUREN • TIFFANY LANIER • DONALD LAREW • J. LARRY LINARES • DAVID LARSON • JACK LASPADA JR. • JASMINE LASSITER • RICK LAUB • JAYNE LAUBE-NELSON • NICK LAUERMAN • LAURENCE LAURENT • JULIE LAURITZEN • MICHAEL LAVIOLETTE • GRANT LAWRENCE • ROBIN LAWRENCE • DANIEL LAWSON • DAVID LAWSON • JOHN LAWSON • ANNE LAZEBNIK • LISA LE • AARON LEBOVIC • DOUGLAS LEDERMAN • CEDRIC LEE • HERMAN LEE • JACKIE LEE • JASON LEE • KEF LEE • LARRY LEE • MIKE LEE • NORMA LEE • VONG LEE • JASON LEEDS • LLOYD LEEK • JOHN LELETZOPOULOS • STEVE LEMBERG • DANIEL LEMIEUX • LORENA LEON • JOHN LEONE • GREGORY LESTER • HARVEY LETSON • JULIA LEVINE • JONAH LEVY • TRACEY LEVY • AMANDA LEWAN • DAVE LEWIS • JOHN LEWIS • ANNA LI • DERVIS LICI • GARY LIDDIARD JR. • KEVIN LIEBETREU • JON LIECKFELT

• VINCE LOPEZ • VINCENT LOPEZ • ERNEST LOPEZ JR. • GUY LORET DE MOLA • ROBERT LORING JR. • ANDREW LOSTUMO • CHRISTOPHER LOVEDAY • JOHN LOVELESS SR. • PHILLIP LOWE • DAVID LOWERY • DAVID LOWING • MATTHEW LOWING • NELLY LOWRIE • KATHERINE LUCAS • POLLY LUCKE • SCOTT LUKOWSKI • BENNY LUMPKINS JR. • COCO LURZ • VICTORIA LURZ • JOSEPH LYMAN • JEFFREY LYNCH • DEBBIE LYNN SIEGEL • CHRISTOPHER LYONS • JAMES LYONS • MICHELLE MACALUSO • JAMES MACDONALD • JOSE MACIAS • MORGAN MACKEW • JOHN MACKLEM • SEAN MACKLER • WILLIAM MACLEOD • CHANDLER MACOCHA • JOHN MACULEVICZ • LARRY MADRID • JOSEPH MAGEE • KRISTA MAGGARD • KATHERINE MAGILL • BRETT MAGNUSON • JASON MAHAKIAN • JULIANNE MAIELLO • JUSTIN MAJED • DAN MAJZLIK • PAUL MALETICH • ERNEST MALIK • MELIK MALKASIAN • BROOKE MALLON • MATTHEW MALLON • STEVE MALLORY • AUGUST MALLOS • CHRISTOPHER MALONE • SARA MALSTROM • JOHN MANFREDI • KEVIN MANGAN • KATIE MANN • CAROLYN MANSER • WARREN MANSER • CHARLES MANSFIELD • MITCH MANSFIELD • DAVID MANSOUR • ERIC MANUEL • LISA MARAHIEL • ALICIA MARIE CLARK • BARBARA MARKO • ELIZABET MARKOSYAN • KEVIN MARKS • KIM MARKS • JEFF MARKWITH • SCOTT MARLATT • DAVID MARR • JOHN MARRA • ED MARSH • DAVE MARSHALL • ELIZABETH MARSHALL • ANDREW MARTI • ALISSA MARTIN • JENNIFER MARTIN • MICHELLE MARTIN • RANCE MARTIN • TIM MARTIN • ARTHUR MARTINEZ • VICTOR MARTINEZ • ROBERT MARTINEZ JR. • TARI MASA • JORDAN MASEK • CLARKE MASON • CRAIG MASON • STEPHANIE MASON • DAVID MASURE-BOSCO • CHRISTOPHER MATHEWS • ROBIN MATHEWS • FRANCES MATHIAS •

SET DECORATOR NANCY HAIGH inspects her work on the set of Oz's trailer.

OTT • JONATHAN OVERGAUUW • REED OVERSTREET • WILLARD OVERSTREET • BRIAN PACE • KYLE PACEK • NATALIE PADILLA • JERRY PAFFENDORF • DAVID PAGE • LOUIS PAGE • ERICA PALAY • ANTONIO PALAZZO • FELICE PAPPAS • JOHN PAPSIDERA • DAN PARCHETA • JOSEPH PARISE • HEATHER PARK • JIYAE PARK • RICHARD PARKINSON • DAVID PARKS • MIKE PARKS • RYAN PARKS • MAXINE PARSHALL • HAROLD PARSON • CRYSTLE PARTINGTON • JOHN PARUCH • RICHARD PASIEKA • BRITTANY PASK • MARK PASKELL • DAVID PASQUESI • CHRISTOPHER PASS • JEFFREY PASSANANTE • MARIO PASSERA • MAREK PATER • DEBORAH PATINO RUTHERFORD • JACOB PATRICK • MARIA PATSALIS • EMILY PATTERSON • SHELLEY PATTERSON • BRANDON PAXTON • JOHN PAXTON •

(LEFT TO RIGHT) SPI Animation Supervisor Troy Saliba, Animatic Artist Jeremy Thompson, VFX Supervisor Scott Stokdyk, Editor Bob Murawski, and Storyboard Artists Mark Vena and David Lowery. Photograph by Merie Wallace.

LARRY PAYNE • PAUL PEABODY • DANIEL PEALY • STEPHANIE PEARL • PAUL PEARSON • BRENT PEDERSON • ZIGGY PEDONE • JESSICA PEEL • RHODA PELL • JOHN PELLEGRINO • DEREK PENDLETON • SYNDERELA PENG • BRIAN PENIKAS • LINDSAY PEPPER • DARIO PEREZ • RAUL PEREZ • JEFFERY PERKINS • LOREN PERONI • BRAD PERSON • GIANLUCA PESCE • NEDA PESUT • ROBERT PETCH • JAMES PETERS • WENDY PETERS • CASEY PETERSON • JESSICA PETRIK • STEPHEN PETRY • MARK PEWARCHIE • MICHAEL PFEIFER • MATT PHILLIBEN • DANIEL PHILLIPS • ELIZABETH PHILLIPS • GABRIELLE PHILLIPS • NOEL PHILLIPS • SARA PHILPOTT • LINDA PHUNG BERMAN • TEDDY PHUTHANHDANH • JESSE PICKERILL • ERIC PICKETT • EDUARDO PIEDRA • TODD PIEPENBROK • CHANNING PIERCE • ADAM PINKSTAFF • RON PIPES JR. • CLAY PLATNER II • STUART PLETCHER • DAN PLUMMER • MASON PODHORSKY • JOE PODNAR JR. • MATTHEW POERTNER • DAVID POLHAMUS • BAO POLKOWSKI • CASEY POND • GEORGE PONSFORD • ANDREW POSKIE • PAUL POSTAL • COLIN POTTS • ERIC POTTS • EVAN POUGNET • LINSIE POULIOT • STACY POULIOT • SCOTT POWELL • CALLIE POWERS • DANIEL POZDOL • JASON PRAET • RACHEL PREISEL • MARGARET PRENTICE • DAVID PRESSMAN • NELLIE PRESTINE-LOWERY • SIVORN PRICE • BENJAMIN PROCTER • STEPHEN PROUTY • IVAN PUENTE • DEBORAH PUETTE • MADDIE PURVIS • GWENDOLYN PYLE • VICTOR PYTKO • AFERDITA QAFA • DONNELL QUAKER • BRADLEY QUICK • CHRIS QUICK • TIMOTHY QUILL • JOR'EL QUINN • TOMMY QUINN • RAUL QUINTANA • TARA QUIST • ELIZABETH RABE • SCOTT RABIDEAU • CHRISTOPHER RABY • L. RACER RANGEL • RICHARD RADOMSKI • JARED RADTKE • JORDAN RAFAEL • DANIELLE RAGLAND • ABRAM RAHAMAN

• ROBERT RAHM • DASHIELL RAIMI • EMMA RAIMI • HENRY RAIMI • OLIVER RAIMI • SAM RAIMI • TED RAIMI • KEVIN RAKES • MELVIN RANDOLPH • BRUCE RASHER • SAHIR RASHID • KATIE RATLIFF • ERIC RAWLS • RENE RAYES • BRITTANY RAYMOND • NICK READE • JOSH REAMES • CRAIG REARDON • TERRY REDDING • RICHARD REDLEFSEN • PATRICK REDMOND • RAYMOND REED • DOUG REED • ANDREW REEDER • DANA REES • JEFFREY REEVES • JAY REID • ROBIN REILLY • TI REN • RAYES RENE • JEFFREY RESSLER • DAVID REVEL • JOSEPH REY • ALEX REYES • SANTOS REYES JR. • ALEX REYNOLDS • JAMES REYNOLDS • KEATON REYNOLDS • KEYNA REYNOLDS • MERRILEE REYNOLDS • SASHA REYNOLDS • ALEJANDRO REYNOSO • LEE RHADIGAN • THOMAS RHADIGAN • BOBBY RHODES • ERIC RHODES • JOHNNY RICE • JONATHON RICE • WENDELL RICE JR. • AARON RICHARDS • STEVE RICHARDSON • ROBERT RICKETTS • DANIELLE RIDGEWAY-JACKSON • MICHAEL RIEGLE • NIKCO RIESGO • JOEL RILEY • KRISTIN RILEY • DIANE RIMAR • ANTHONY RINALDI • PETER RINEHART • JENNIFER RINGRESS • DEAN RINKE • JESSICA RIPKA • GEOFF RIST • CHRISTOPHER RITTER • JENNA RITTER • NICK RITZ • FELIX RIVERA • RACHEL RIVERA • ANTHONY RIVERA JR. • SVETLANA RIVKINA • LINDA RIZZUTO • DEREEK ROBERSON • FRANCIS ROBERT • MARK ROBERTS • TERRI ROBERTSON • ARES ROBINSON • ALAN ROBITAILLE • JASON ROBY • CASEY ROCHE • RYAN ROCHE • JOSEPH RODMELL • ALEX RODRIGUEZ • PATRICIO RODRIGUEZ • RICHARD RODRIGUEZ • RYEN RODRIGUEZ • ANDREA ROGERS • BILL ROGERS • ERIK ROGERS • JIM ROGERS • MEGHAN ROGERS • SCOTT ROGERS • TED ROGERS • SPENCER ROHAN • WILIAN ROMAGOZA • ADAM ROMANO • CAROL ROONEY • CHRISTOPHER ROSE • ERIC ROSE • JENNA ROSE • NATALIE ROSE KAUFFMAN • JOE ROSS • JENNIFER ROSSINI • JAMES ROTHROCK • ELIE ROTHSTEIN • JENNA ROTHSTEIN • DENNIS ROTTELL • CAROLINE ROURKE • PATRICK ROUSSEAU • SANDRA ROWDEN • CHRISTOPHER ROWE • DANNY ROWE JR. • CANDICE ROWLAND • THOMAS ROY • SARAH RUBANO • JAMES RUBBO • ROSE RUBIN • LUCIANO RUBIO • NICK RUBSENSTEIN • SARAH RUDNICKI •

ROCHELLE RUDOLPH • FRANKLIN RUEHL JR. • MICHELLE RUFF • JOEL RUIZ • KATHLEEN RUNEY • JAN RUONA • SHAUN RUSSELL • TRAVIS RUSSELL • DON RUTHERFORD • CHRISTIAN RUZZUTI • RICHARD RYAN • REAGAN RYSDALE • ADAM RZADOWOSKI • JORDAN SABOURIN • ARI SACHTER-ZELTZER • NEIL SACKS • ANTHONY SAENZ JR. • HILARY SAHN • MATTHEW SAKATA • JAVIER SALDANA • DAIMAN SALDIVAR • GLENN SALLOUM • MARIA SALLOUM • AVA SALMACI • JASON SALZMAN • DOV SAMUEL • KELLY SAMUELS • JOHN SANACORE • HUGO SANCHEZ • PAUL SANCHEZ • WALDO SANCHEZ • ERIC SANDERLIN • JEFFREY SANDERS • JERRY SANDERS • RICHARD SANDERS • NATHAN SANDERSON • ERIC SANDLIN • DENNIS SANDS • ELLEN SANDWEISS • MARK SANGER • ERIC SAPERSTEIN • GREGORY SARACENO • KHALIL SARDY • NICOLE SASS SCHATTLE • MARK SATTERFIELD • MICHAEL SAUNDERS • PATRICIA SAUNDERS • BRENT SAWICKI • CHESTER SAWIKI • ROBERT SAYERS • STACY SAYERS • DEVIN SCANDORE • PATRICK SCANLAN • JOSEPH SCARCELLI • JOHANNAH SCARLET • LAUREN SCHAFER • HENRY SCHAUB • THOMAS SCHELL • BRIAN SCHELTER • HAYLEY SCHILLING • KEITH SCHLOEMP • CHRISTINA SCHMIDT • DAVID SCHMIDT • JAY SCHMIDT • JOHN SCHMIDT • JASON SCHNITZER • CHAD SCHULER • JESSICA SCHULTE • TIM SCHULTES • SCOTT SCHUTZKI • DAVID SCHWAGER • DONALD SCHWALM • JAMES SCHWALM • RICHARD SCHWALM • JAMES SCHWALM JR. • JEFFREY SCHWARTZ • MARK SCHWARZ • FRANK SCHWEIGER JR. • ROBERT SCHWEITZER • WILLIAM SCHWOCHO • ALEXANDER SCOTT • DAVID SCOTT • THOMAS SCOTT • MICHAEL SCOTTY • SARAH SCRIVENER • JOE SCULLY • CARLOS SEALIE • BRIAN SEARLE • DENNIS SEAWRIGHT • KATIE SECOR • ELLEN SEGAL • FRED SEIBLY • MARK SEJNOWSKI • NICHOLAS SEJNOWSKI • MIA SERAFINO • MARIA SERRANO • JONATHAN SESSIONS • MARYN SETSUDA • GINA SETTER • MARY SEWARD-MCKEON • JOE SFAIR • CHRISTOPHER SHADLEY • NIKKI SHAH • IRA SHAIN • CLAYTON SHANK • MARKUM SHANNON • DARRYL SHAW • DESMOND SHAW • JACK SHAW • MK SHAW • BRITTANY SHEA • GEORDIE SHEFFER • CHRISTOPHER SHEFSTAD • JESS SHELTON • ISABELLA SHEPARD • BRIAN SHEVELA • DEREK SHIKWANA • ROBERT SHOBE • JONATHAN SHROYER • JOEL SHRYACK • CARL SHUFFETT • MARY SHUFFETT • JASON SHUPE • STEVEN SHUPICK • PETER SIKKELEE • NATHANIEL SILBERG • JENNIFER SILLS • ASHLEY SILOAC • CRAIG SILVA • DOMENIC SILVESTRI • JAMIE SILVINO • ANTHONY SIMMS • KALEB

SIMOKOVIC • JAMES SIMON • ANGELA SIMPSON • PETER SIMPSON • JASON SINCLAIR • BILL SINISCHO • SHERZAD SINJARI • JOSEPH SIQUEIROS • DAVID SIREIKA JR. • SHERYL SIRMONS • ANDY SISUL • MIRO SKANDERA • LARRY SKINNER • SANDY SKOGLUND • AIDA SLEEPER • SANFORD SLEPAK • JOSHUA SLOAN • PHILIP SLOAN • SAM SLOCUM • ALISON SMITH • BRUCE SMITH • CHARLES SMITH • CHRISTIAN SMITH • CLAY SMITH • EASTON SMITH • NAOMI SMITH • NIKKI SMITH • RICK SMITH • STEPHANIE SMITH • VALENTINO SMITH • ZION SMITH • GREG SMITH ALDRIGE • MARIA SMITH-BYRD • AMY SNELL • LARRY SNELL • ZACHARY SNIDERMAN • ROSLYNNE SNOECK • KENDALL SNOW • DAVID SNUGGS • KATHY SNYDER • KELLY SNYDER • SARAH SNYDER • TOM SNYDER • STEVE SOBASCO • ERIC SOBCZAK • KATRINA SOLOMON • LAUREN SOLOMON • ALEXANDRA SOMAND • STEVE SONG • STEFAN SONNENFELD • SCOTT SOON • ZION SORANI • ALBERT SORENTINO JR. • MARK SOUCIE • DAVID SOUSA • FRANK SPADAFORA • KEITH SPAGNOL • DOMENIC SPALVIER • THOMAS SPARKMAN • MARK SPARKS • PAUL SPEAR • ABIGAIL SPENCER • JERRY SPENCER • MARY SPENCER • CLIFFORD SPERRY • CHRISTOPHER SPICER • DAVID SPIEGELMAN • GEORGE SPIELVOGEL • MICHAEL SPIES • QUINN SPILSBURY • DAVID SPRADLIN • TROY SPROTT • JOHN SPYTKO • SHERI ST LAWRENCE • JOHN STABLEY JR. • MICHELLE STADLER • ANDREW STAHL • GARRETT STAIRS • SHAUN STALLARD • MIRJANA STANAJ • TRAVIS STANBERRY • MICHAEL STANFORD • KENNETH STANLEY • JEFFREY STANTON • KIRK STARBIRD • DAVID STASIAK • CHRIS STATHES • DAN STAYNE • BLAKE STEELGRAVE • SEBASTIEN STELLA • MAUREEN STEMEN • WILLIAM STEPHANOFF • DEVIN STERLING • ETHAN STERN • PHILIP STEUER • QI STEVEN JIN • GEORGE STEVENS • JOSHUA STEVENS • KENNETH STEVENS • PAUL STEVENS • LINDA STEVENSON-KHAN • APRIL STEWART • DOUG STEWART • FREDRICK STIEHR III • DEREK STILL JR. • BOB STILLINGS • ZACHARY STINSON • SARAH STITELER • JOHNNY STOCKARD • THAD STOCKMEYER • SCOTT STODDARD • CLAIRE STONE • JEREMY STONE • RANDALL STONE • KELLIE STONEBROOK • BRETT STORM • JACK STORY • JEFFERY STOUT • SARAH STOUT •

PROPERTY MASTER RUSSELL BOBBITT (right) and James Franco (left) discuss a scene while Tinker Michael Clossin (middle) looks on. Photograph by Merie Wallace.

EARLY OZ OVERLOOK
by Concept Illustrator
Steven Messing.

DIRECTOR SAM RAIMI discusses the day's shoot with Director of Photography Peter Deming and 1st Assistant Director K.C. Hodenfield. Photograph by Merie Wallace.

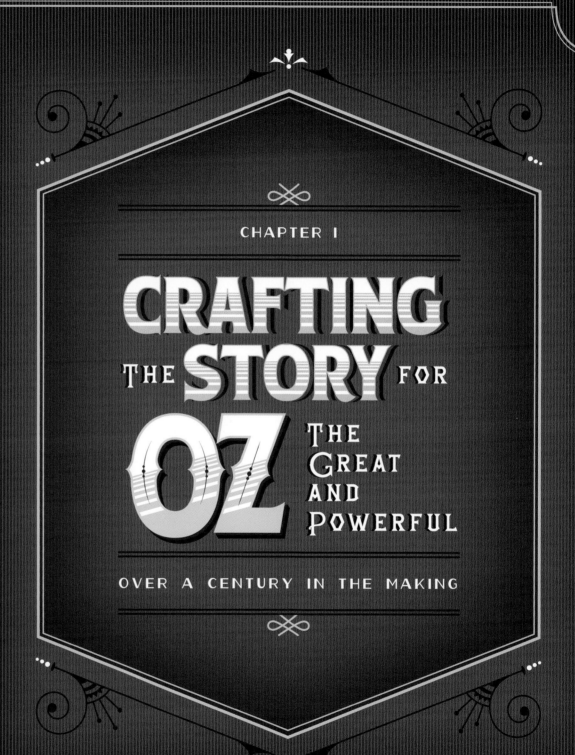

CHAPTER I

CRAFTING THE STORY FOR OZ THE GREAT AND POWERFUL

OVER A CENTURY IN THE MAKING

"L. Frank Baum's books have resonated for over a hundred years. They touch very deep chords about what it means to become independent, what it means to go home, what it means to gather elements of your personality that are missing at the time. Everybody can relate to something in his books."

JOE ROTH, *producer*

ONE **EXTRAORDINARY** LIFE—
ONE **EXTRAORDINARY** IMAGINATION

To faithfully record the trials and triumphs that brought *Oz The Great and Powerful* to the silver screen, one must first understand the trials and triumphs of the man whose whimsical imagination created the Land of Oz, L. Frank Baum.

Lyman Frank Baum was born in Chittenango, New York, on May 15, 1856, to parents Cynthia Stanton and Benjamin Ward Baum. He was the seventh of nine children, four of whom passed away before adulthood.

Interestingly, it was Baum's own childhood health concerns that created the environment that nurtured his love of storytelling. Due to a heart defect, Baum was homeschooled and spent numerous hours in his father's library reading the popular children's fairy tales of the day. However, he was so disillusioned by the violence and scary creatures featured in these stories that he adapted kinder, friendlier versions of the adventures to give to other children.

Baum's father took note of his son's extracurricular narrative activities. Having made a considerable fortune in the oil fields of Pennsylvania, he had the means to indulge in the burgeoning literary interests of his son and purchased a printing press to help him. The press was installed in the family's estate, named Rose Lawn, and soon Baum and a younger brother, Harry, produced the *Rose Lawn Home Journal*, which was replete with advertisements, fiction, poetry, and editorials.

By the time Baum—who went by Frank due to a dislike of his first name—was seventeen, he had another amateur journal under his belt, *Baum's Complete Stamp Dealers Directory*. This publication was the result of his interest in a new fad at the time, stamp collecting, and led to a stamp dealership that he started with his friends.

L. FRANK BAUM

Baum's interest in the fads of the day, coupled with his strong writing skills and entrepreneurship acumen, turned out to be a perfect foundation for his future endeavors. He melded them all together again at the age of twenty when the craze of breeding fancy poultry swept the nation. The particular breed of chicken that held Baum's attention was the Hamburg, and he soon began publishing *The Poultry Record*. His success in breeding the bird led him to be the founder of the Empire State Poultry Association. Additionally, Baum's poultry prowess eventually spawned his first published book, *The Book of the Hamburgs: A Brief Treatise Upon the Mating, Rearing and Management of the Different Varieties of Hamburgs*.

Frank enjoyed rearing Hamburgs, but by the time he was twenty-five a new love entered his life— theater. As was the case with the printing press, his father's fortune and generosity provided the means from which the younger Baum was able to showcase his talents. Benjamin Baum constructed a playhouse for his son in Richburg, New York, where Frank wrote, produced, composed the music for, and starred in numerous productions of his own plays.

As Baum's affection for the theater blossomed, so to did his love for a young woman he met named Maud Gage, the daughter of a famous women's rights activist, Matilda Gage. On November 9, 1882, the pair married and formed a union that would last until Frank's passing over thirty-six years later.

While Baum's marriage would stand the test of time, his Richburg theater unfortunately would not. As he was touring with one of the productions of his play *The Maid of Arran*, the theater caught fire during a performance of his fatefully titled *Matches*, and Baum's theatrical career literally went up in flames.

At this point in his life, Baum's entrepreneurial urges got the best of him and he and Maud moved to Aberdeen, South Dakota, to open a general store called Baum's Bazaar. Sadly, the establishment proved to be a failure, as did his stint editing *The Aberdeen Saturday Pioneer*, a local newspaper.

W. W. DENSLOW CYCLONE
artwork from *The Wonderful Wizard of Oz.*

After Baum's disappointments in South Dakota, he and Maud moved to the Humboldt Park section of Chicago. However, it was now more challenging for Baum to indulge in his fancies, as they came back financially drained and with four boys in tow. While in Chicago, Baum took on a series of odd jobs to try and reestablish a monetary foundation. He was a reporter for *The Evening Post*, edited a magazine for advertising agencies focused on in-store window displays, and was a traveling salesman for porcelain and crockery manufacturers.

Fortunately for children and parents in need of kinder, friendlier fairy tales, none of these vocations provided fulfillment and Baum's creative juices forced their way to the surface. At night he would tell his sons fanciful tales, some of which his mother-in-law Matilda, now a live-in, would overhear. She encouraged Frank to write them down, and Baum did so in the form of a children's book, *Mother Goose in Prose*. The book contained twenty-two tales, the last one of which interestingly introduces a heroine named Dorothy. The collection was good enough to attract a publisher, and in 1897 Baum was back on a literary track.

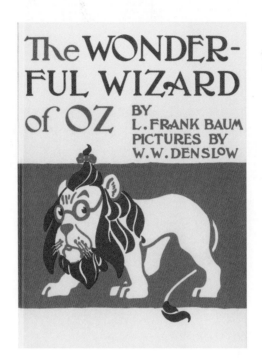

Mother Goose in Prose was successful enough that Baum was able to write full time. Untethered, Baum penned *Father Goose, His Book*, which was published in 1899. It went on to sell an estimated 175,000 copies and became the best-selling children's book of the year.

In addition to the financial and literary success *Father Goose, His Book* ushered in, it also introduced him to illustrator W. W. Denslow, who would be a key collaborator on Baum's next children's narrative effort, *The Wonderful Wizard of Oz*.

(CLOCKWISE FROM TOP RIGHT) Illustrator W. W. Denslow and the cover art from his first two collaborations with Baum.

The Wonderful Wizard of Oz was published on May 17, 1900, by George M. Hill Company and contained 154 original W. W. Denslow illustrations of the universe Baum had created within. It was greeted with instant success and was the first in a series of fourteen Oz books that cemented Baum's literary legacy.

However, immediately following Baum's inaugural Oz offering, he chose to pen stories outside the land that had made him famous. In 1901 he published *Dot and Tot in Merryland,* as well as his science fiction entry, *The Master Key.* The next year, 1902, heralded Baum's take on the Christmas legend with *The Adventures of Santa Claus.*

It would not be until 1903 that Baum would return to Oz, albeit in theatrical, not book, form. Immediately following the publication of *The Wonderful Wizard of Oz* in 1900, Baum and Denslow adapted their tale for the stage along with composer Paul Tietjens and director Julian Mitchell. However, it wasn't until 1903 that their play, whose title had been shortened to *The Wizard of Oz,* made it to Broadway and enjoyed an intermittent, yet successful, run until December 1904.

That same year, the literary rebirth of the Land of Oz came with the publication of *The Marvelous Land of Oz.* Like its predecessor, it was popular, and just like Baum's maiden voyage into Oz, it came at a time of fiscal need.

Although Baum had seen monetary success with *The Wonderful Wizard of Oz* and its Broadway adaptation, his follow-up books outside of Oz were not as profitable. Likewise, he continued to mount plays based on his work, but none of these endeavors proved to be a financial boon. Thus began a pattern that would continue for years to come—Baum's attempts to write and create outside the Land of Oz his fans clamored and paid for, and his need to be drawn back into said world due to ongoing financial missteps.

(TOP) Denslow's rendition of Glinda the Good Witch meeting with Dorothy and friends.

(BOTTOM) Denslow's title page artwork from *The Wonderful Wizard of Oz.*

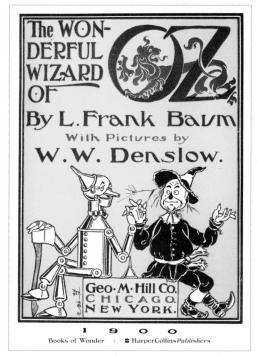

A FLYING MONKEY, as envisioned by Denslow from the pages of *The Wonderful Wizard of Oz*.

Baum was so intent on parting ways with the fictitious franchise that at the end of book six, *The Emerald City of Oz*, published in 1910, one of the final paragraphs is a note from Dorothy that reads:

> *You will never hear anything more about Oz, because we are now cut off forever from all the rest of the world. But Toto and I will always love you and all the other children who love us.*
> —Dorothy Gale

Baum echoed Dorothy's message in the final two paragraphs of the book when he penned his own farewell to the series:

> *This seemed to me too bad, at first, for Oz is a very interesting fairyland. Still, we have no right to feel grieved, for we have had enough of the history of the Land of Oz to fill six story books, and from its quaint people and their strange adventures we have been able to learn many useful and amusing things.*

> *So good luck to little Dorothy and her companions. May they live long in their invisible country and be very happy!*

As Baum waved good-bye to Dorothy, in the coming years he said hello to bankruptcy, failing health, and a sextet of books—*The Daring Twins* (1911), *The Sea Fairies* (1911), *Sky Island* (1912), *Phoebe Daring* (1912), *Our Married Life* (1912), and *Johnson* (1912)—that failed to generate adequate sales. As a result, Baum, who by this time had relocated his clan to Hollywood, California, needed to continue journaling the various adventures that took place within the Land of Oz in order to make ends meet. But he had closed the door on the series to such a degree that it proved to be a daunting narrative challenge. The Land of Oz was now invisible and no messages were allowed in or out. However, Baum was a visionary at heart, and he easily surmounted this obstacle by opening book seven in the Oz series, *The Patchwork Girl of Oz*, with:

> *. . . So the Historian rigged up a high tower in his back yard, and took lessons in wireless telegraphy until he understood it, and then began to call Princess Dorothy of Oz by sending messages into the air.*

Now, it wasn't likely that Dorothy would be looking for wireless messages or would heed the call; but one thing the Historian was sure of, and that was that the powerful Sorceress, Glinda the Good Witch of the South, would know what he was doing and that he desired to communicate with Dorothy. For Glinda has a big book in which is recorded every event that takes place anywhere in the world, just the moment that it happens, and so of course the book would tell her about the wireless message.

And that was the way Dorothy heard that the Historian wanted to speak with her . . . and the Historian begged so hard to be told the latest news of Oz, so that he could write it down for the children to read, that Dorothy asked permission of Ozma and Ozma graciously consented.

That is why, after two long years of waiting, another Oz story is now presented to the children of America. This would not have been possible had not some clever man invented the "wireless" and an equally clever child suggested the idea of reaching the mysterious Land of Oz by its means. —L. Frank Baum

After the release of *The Patchwork Girl of Oz* in 1913, Baum wrote a new Oz adventure every year until he passed away on May 6, 1919, due to a stroke. All told, Baum penned fourteen adventures that took place in Oz; two of them, *The Magic of Oz* (1919) and *Glinda of Oz* (1920), were published posthumously.

DENSLOW illustration featuring The Guardian of the Gates from *The Wonderful Wizard of Oz*.

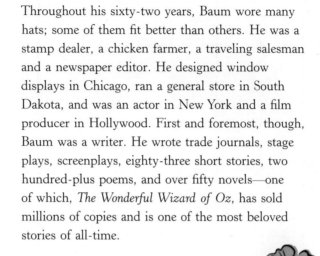

Throughout his sixty-two years, Baum wore many hats; some of them fit better than others. He was a stamp dealer, a chicken farmer, a traveling salesman and a newspaper editor. He designed window displays in Chicago, ran a general store in South Dakota, and was an actor in New York and a film producer in Hollywood. First and foremost, though, Baum was a writer. He wrote trade journals, stage plays, screenplays, eighty-three short stories, two hundred-plus poems, and over fifty novels—one of which, *The Wonderful Wizard of Oz*, has sold millions of copies and is one of the most beloved stories of all-time.

To fully understand the impact Baum made during his lifetime, perhaps one only has to look as far as one of his own quotes from 1917's *The Lost Princess of Oz*:

Imagination has brought mankind through the Dark Ages to its present state of civilization. Imagination led Columbus to discover America. Imagination led Franklin to discover electricity. Imagination has given us the steam engine, the telephone, the talking-machine and the automobile, for these had to be dreamed of before they became realities. So I believe that dreams—daydreams, you know, with your eyes wide open and your brain-machinery whizzing—are likely to lead to the betterment of the world. The imaginative child will become the imaginative man or woman most apt to create, to invent, and therefore to foster civilization. —L. Frank Baum

AN ORIGINAL DENSLOW illustration of the poppy fields, showing the effects of its everlasting sleep enchantment.

It STARTED With a QUESTION

Baum's musings on the whimsical world of Oz and the colorful characters within have managed to weave themselves into the fabric of our culture and inspired numerous visionaries to interpret and expound upon his creation. One such storyteller is Mitchell Kapner who tried numerous times to get his story set in the Land of Oz off the ground in Hollywood.

"I had always loved the idea of asking, 'How did the Wizard become the Wizard?' and the interesting narrative possibilities that question instigated," states Kapner. "For years, I would go into general meetings with producers and studio executives and they'd say, 'Do you have any passion projects?' And I would say, 'I've always wanted to tell the story of how the Wizard became the Wizard.' And the response I'd always get was, 'Thank you very much, good-bye.' After awhile I simply stopped pitching it."

For years Kapner refrained from mentioning Baum's land in meetings. However, a July 31, 2009, conversation with *Oz The Great and Powerful* executive producer Palak Patel, the president of legendary filmmaker Joe Roth's production company, changed that.

"Mitchell first came in on a general meeting," comments Patel. "He pitched me a number of things, and then we started talking about how he was reading L. Frank Baum's books to his children at night. And he said, 'Did you ever think about doing a story on how the Wizard became the Wizard?' I knew he was onto something with that question. Baum had created such a magnificent world with dozens and dozens of characters and fantastical set pieces."

Kapner and Patel continued to discuss the Land of Oz, and at the end of the meeting Mitchell received a response that he had waited years to hear. "Palak looked at me," recalls Kapner, "and said, 'I love that. Joe's gonna love that. Let's do it.'"

SCREENWRITER Mitchell Kapner on one of the sets for *Oz The Great and Powerful.* Photograph by Merie Wallace.

A meeting was promptly scheduled with *Oz The Great and Powerful* producer Joe Roth, and Palak's prediction was spot-on. Having produced *Alice in Wonderland*, and being in development on *Snow White and the Huntsman* at the time, Roth knew the attraction of Baum's fantasy world. "Fairy-tale movies resonate because they are stories that are hundreds and hundreds of years old most of the time," comments Roth. "They've been translated into every language, to every generation. There's something in their core that really speaks to people."

In addition to *Alice in Wonderland* and *Snow White and the Huntsman*, Roth has produced over fifty films, directed six, and guided literally hundreds of movies from script to screen during his tenures as chairman of Twentieth Century Fox (1989–1993) and Walt Disney Studios (1994–2000). Roth's experience with storytelling, in particular his fondness for origin stories, was one of the aspects of Kapner's initial pitch that ultimately piqued his interest. "Mitchell's notion was, 'Who is the Wizard and how did he get there?'" states Roth. "It was a great place to start."

(TOP) Producer Joe Roth takes in the 3-D sites on the set of *Oz The Great and Powerful*.

(BOTTOM) Production Designer Robert Stromberg and Executive Producer Palak Patel. Photographs by Merie Wallace

ORIGINAL EMERALD CITY cityscape by W. W. Denslow.

With one of Baum's most iconic characters as their lead, and his extraordinary world of Oz as the backdrop, the trio set about creating the story line and circumstances that put Oscar Diggs, also known as Oz, into the Emerald City. Commenting on the overall vision that emerged from these initial meetings, Patel states, "We wanted a definitive version of the story of Oz that Baum would be proud of if he were still alive today, while staying true to all the characters and story lines that he had in his books."

To pen such a definitive version, at this juncture Kapner spent numerous hours studying Baum's adventures and becoming an expert on the Land of Oz. "Mitchell earned his PhD in Oz," says Patel. "He read every single book four or five times over. He knew every character, every story line." Adds Roth, "Mitchell was an expert on the Baum books. He was constantly referring back to the various stories. No one knows that catalog better than he does."

During this period of intense study, one thing became clear to Kapner: there was not a definitive book, or even a chapter, on how Diggs became the Wizard. The story that he, Roth, and Patel wanted to spin took place before book one in Baum's odyssey, which had the Wizard already ruling the Land of Oz. "There are only about four paragraphs in all of the books about how the Wizard became the Wizard," explains Kapner. "That gave me a lot of leeway."

Additionally, the early *Oz The Great and Powerful* blueprint included another witch, Glinda the Good Witch of the South. Unlike her wicked counterparts, she plays a central role in many of the journeys that take place in Baum's Oz. Nevertheless, there is a scarce amount of material written on her origins. Thus, another character development opportunity presented itself to Kapner, Roth, and Patel.

As they started connecting the dots, some present in Baum's books and some fabricated, the overall story really fell into place. "We started the process by developing the character of Oz and outlining the journey his character embarked upon. We then went in and focused on Theodora, Evanora, and Glinda—creating the witches and what their motivation was, what their backstory was," comments Patel. "After working all this out with Mitchell, we knew we had something pretty amazing on our hands. We had the origin story of the Wizard, and the witches, that takes place thirty years before Dorothy ever stepped foot in Oz. All of which takes place from the point of view of the Wizard as a young man. It echoed Kapner's first pitch—it was how Oz became the Wizard."

GLINDA THE GOOD WITCH and Dorothy depart after the end of the grand adventures in *The Wonderful Wizard of Oz.*

There was another key discovery made during this early exploration that presented an additional opportunity for origin stories. In Baum's tales, there is precious little mentioned about the Wicked Witch of the East and the Wicked Witch of the West. However, they played key roles in the early blueprint that had emerged for *Oz The Great and Powerful.* "In the books, the Wicked Witch of the East is dead the whole time, and the Wicked Witch of the West appears sporadically in the first half of book one, and then she dies," recounts Kapner.

By mid-August 2009, this collaborative development process had birthed a twelve-page treatment and the conversation turned to which movie studio would be the best home at which to make the film. One name was at the top of that list—Disney.

"Disney was the perfect place to make the film because Baum's epic in today's world is a Disney movie," states Roth. "There are so many wonderful characters, fascinating lands, hundreds of creatures—this was a Disney movie." Patel seconds Roth's sentiment. "Disney has such a rich history of doing these kinds of stories that are for children and adults. This story is a mixture of great character, great emotion, and amazing set pieces for the kids, and an unbelievably imaginative and fantastical world. No one does it better than Disney, and so in our minds it was always the first place that we wanted to go."

A mid-August meeting was scheduled with Roth, Patel, Kapner, and then-president of production, Oren Aviv. "It was the most nervous I've been before starting a pitch," recalls Kapner. "I knew this was the opportunity of a lifetime." Aviv also recognized the opportunity and liked the pitch. On August 28, 2009, Kapner's deal to write the screenplay officially closed.

With a deal in place and a solid overall story mapped out, Kapner retreated to his home office to write the screenplay to the temporarily titled *Brick*. Baum's tales are in the public domain, meaning anyone can make an Oz movie, and numerous companies were attempting to do so. Therefore, the team decided to keep "Oz" out of the title for as long as possible to refrain from tipping their hand to the Hollywood community.

DENSLOW'S Guard of the Gate.

The fall of 2009 saw Kapner delicately blending what little was known about Oscar Diggs from Baum, and the revelations that emerged from the whirlwind of executive meetings that had transpired during the previous months. Oz was known to be a magician and a fraud from the books, but as Kapner typed away, other aspects of his personality presented themselves.

"Oz wants to be great. He doesn't want to settle," comments Mitchell about some of the blanks he filled in. "He watched his father die a poor dirt farmer, and he will do whatever it takes to get to the next level and avoid the same fate. And in the process, he's probably pushing people away." As Oz's character came into focus in script form, so did Kapner's fascination with the witches. "I was very interested in the sister dynamic we created between the Wicked Witch of the East, named Evanora, and the Wicked Witch of the West, Theodora," he says. "I loved how they played off each other—the push, the pull, the manipulation, the little secrets they had. And then there was Glinda the Good Witch of the South and her impact on that dynamic. I liked that Theodora was between Glinda and Evanora. She's pulled by both sides."

The intricacies of the various relationships and story lines continued to gel for Kapner, and on February 12, 2010, he handed over his first draft of *Oz The Great and Powerful* to Roth and Patel. The duo loved how the characters and the story had progressed from treatment to script and subsequently sent the screenplay to Sean Bailey, who had recently been named president of production at Disney, and executive vice president of production Brigham Taylor. They agreed with Roth and Patel's assessment and the project leapfrogged its way from pitch to priority in a scant six months after finding a home at Disney.

"IF **THIS** WAS **EASY,** WE **WOULDN'T** NEED A **WIZARD, WOULD** WE?"

Not only are these poignant lines Michelle Williams delivers as Glinda the Good Witch of the South, they also point out a key component the project lacked at this juncture—a visionary director, a wizard, who could hone the script and marry the resulting narrative components to a fantastical world worthy of the Oz lineage. As the search for such a wizard began, one name rose to the top: Sam Raimi.

"Everything made Sam Raimi the right director for this movie," comments Roth. "He's worked on films this size, which is large. He's worked in a world of special effects and live action combined. There are very few of those directors. And more than anything, he has the heart and sensibility of the story."

As Roth points out, the list of directors who can juggle both story and spectacle at the same time is few and far between. Add Raimi's numerous other filmmaking talents to the mix, and the unique vision he brings to a film becomes readily apparent. Not only has Raimi helmed fourteen films— including the Spider-Man and Evil Dead trilogies, *A Simple Plan,* and *The Gift*—he's also produced over thirty films and television shows; created memorable characters in front of the camera as an actor; and has written more than ten films and television shows, including *The Hudsucker Proxy* with the Coen brothers.

"Sam is one of the few filmmakers that we have today in modern cinema that combines the savvy technical aspects of filmmaking, mixing it with great emotion and character-driven storytelling," says Patel. "At heart, he is a man who is all about story, all about character. But behind all that, he knows how to put on the greatest show ever."

At the encouragement of Raimi's wife, Gillian; his agent at Creative Artists Agency, Craig Gering; and an executive at his production company, Russell Hollander, Raimi took a peek at Kapner's script and fell in love with it.

DIRECTOR SAM RAIMI holds a key prop from the film, Oz's music box. Photograph by Merie Wallace.

"Mitchell took me on a ride. I was engaged with his vision, and the vision of L. Frank Baum, and I really just saw the film the way they told it as writers," remarks Raimi. "It had a great main character that I really liked and connected with. The adventure Oz went on was fun, and the story had an uplifting quality I thoroughly enjoyed. I love when movies are uplifting, and I thought this would make a great fantasy film for all audiences."

Raimi signed on shortly thereafter and Kapner was ecstatic. "I could feel my skin tingle," admits Kapner. "I just knew he was the absolute right guy in terms of a director who can deliver on the heart and soul of a piece, but also orchestrate those 'popcorn' moments that wow the audience."

By July 2010, Raimi and Kapner were meeting in the production offices that had been set up at Tribeca West in Los Angeles for *Oz The Great and Powerful*. *Brick* had since been jettisoned, because with the addition of Raimi, the project was no longer flying under Hollywood's radar. Paramount on Raimi's narrative to-do list with Kapner was accentuating Oz's character motivations. "I loved that this was the story of how the Wizard became the Wizard—how he was a small-time magician, a faker, a charlatan—who came to this fantastical world and was just the ingredient they needed to save the day," observes Raimi. "I also really wanted to focus on another wonderful aspect of Mitchell's script—at its core, it's the story of how an average man who was selfish became a great wizard who was selfless."

(LEFT) Director Sam Raimi laughs while directing a scene. Photograph by Merie Wallace.

(RIGHT) Oz looks down upon the fantastical Land of Oz as featured in *The Wonderful Wizard of Oz*.

SCREENWRITER
David Lindsay-Abaire.
Photograph by Merie Wallace.

The addition of David Lindsay-Abaire proved a perfect fit and was paying dividends in the form of new script pages by the fall of 2010. "David's strengths are character, emotion, relationships, complexity, and story lines," explains Patel. "He worked from the foundation that Mitchell created, and enhanced it along with Sam."

Lindsay-Abaire elaborates on the creative exploration he embarked upon with Raimi: "Sam is the most respectful film director that I've worked with. He's so incredibly collaborative and open and genuinely interested in my opinion. I'm mostly a playwright, which is a very collaborative process. It's refreshing to me to have that similar process in film. The script is a breathing thing that's always evolving. Sam's process makes the story sharper and all the better because of it."

Kapner and Raimi set about this task alongside Pulitzer Prize-winning playwright (*Rabbit Hole*) and screenwriter David Lindsay-Abaire. Raimi had collaborated with Lindsay-Abaire on multiple projects along with his producing partners Josh Donen and Grant Curtis, who were onboard *Oz The Great and Powerful* by this time.

"The stories that Sam and I tell tend to be driven by character and emotion," comments Lindsay-Abaire. "I loved the world that had been created. I loved the characters. The raw material was so rich and present that it made my job much easier."

On January 4, 2011, this collaboration produced a full script. "In our collective version of the story, what I love the most about the character of Oz is that he was such a dastardly heel, but he craved something greater, both from his life, but also from himself as a person. He's such an iconic character and we worked really hard to make him human," states Lindsay-Abaire. "He wanted to do great things, and he starts the story thinking being great is one thing—money, power, riches—and by the end of the story, he finds out it's actually about making connections and finding love and friendship."

THE MUNCHKINS as originally envisioned by W. W. Denslow.

In the period between David's first submission and the first day of principal photography, July 21, 2011, the script would receive a variety of tweaks as preproduction advanced. Meetings were held with Kapner, Lindsay-Abaire, Raimi, Roth, Patel, Donen, Curtis, Bailey, Taylor, and Disney director of production Tonia Davis in which some story lines were expanded upon, while others shrank or disappeared all together. Additionally, characters were added, some were removed and lie in wait to join future potential adventures, and others remained but with a new moniker. Furthermore, financial considerations inevitably presented themselves and certain locations were downsized, a few were combined, and one or two found themselves on the chopping block. But as the story naturally evolved, its heart and soul remained intact.

At its core, *Oz The Great and Powerful* is the story of a selfish man who becomes selfless while in a land of second chances. Baum created the man and the land, but a simple question—"How did the Wizard became the Wizard?"—planted the seed from which a new Oz adventure grew.

CHAPTER II

DESIGNING

THE LAND OF OZ

THE GREAT AND POWERFUL

WALT DISNEY'S CLASSICS LIVE ON

"Creating the world of Oz is the biggest creative challenge we've ever had to face."

SAM RAIMI, *director*

"When I started designing the Land of Oz, I felt a little bit like Oscar Diggs himself. I just sort of stumbled into what it became. There's no rule book for creating these worlds. You just have to sit down and start playing with the design. You discover it along the way and build it up over time. For me personally, there is no other outlet of creativity I can think of that even approaches this scale. That's part of what I love about this job."

ROBERT STROMBERG, *production designer*

ONCE UPON A TIME

In some ways, designing the look of *Oz The Great and Powerful* began over a century ago, emerging from L. Frank Baum's pen and William Wallace Denslow's brush. Baum's vivid descriptions of the Land of Oz and its odd inhabitants gave his readers a detailed picture of the world that housed the epic adventures his characters embarked upon. His text, coupled with the distinctive illustrations of Denslow, who went by W. W., ushered young and old alike into a land populated by evil witches, flying monkeys, and a strange old man named Oz.

In many ways however, the creative building blocks that would breathe life into Oz, as seen in *Oz The Great and Powerful*, fell into place throughout the 1960s and '70s as filmmaker William R. Stromberg passed on his love for early Disney animation and miniatures to his artistically gifted son, Robert.

"Because of my dad, I became a huge fan of the classic Disney films—*Sleeping Beauty, Bambi, Pinocchio*," recalls production designer Robert Stromberg. "When I was a kid, I had a huge book on Disney called *The Art of Walt Disney*. I remember it had Mickey Mouse holding a paintbrush on the front cover. I used to draw every picture in that book. I'd then show my father these images and he would encourage me to do more. I know Disney classic art like the back of my hand."

Stromberg's creative upbringing and his love for film led to a career that began in the 1980s as a matte painter, and quickly advanced to that of a visual effects supervisor and designer, working on such films as, *The Aviator, Memoirs of a Geisha, There Will Be Blood,* and *Tropic Thunder.*

COVER from the book *The Art of Walt Disney.* The illustrations within inspired some design aspects of *Oz The Great and Powerful.*

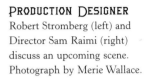

PRODUCTION DESIGNER
Robert Stromberg (left) and
Director Sam Raimi (right)
discuss an upcoming scene.
Photograph by Merie Wallace.

As Robert's list of credits grew, so did his reputation
as someone at the forefront of digital world creation.
His creative emergence coincided with writer/
director/producer James Cameron's need to envision
the world of Pandora for his film *Avatar*. Along
with legendary production designer Rick Carter,
Cameron enlisted the services of Stromberg, and
the inspired pairing led to a 2010 Academy Award
for their groundbreaking vision. The following year
Stromberg again took Oscar home for production
design for his innovative work on Tim Burton's *Alice
in Wonderland*.

Oz The Great and Powerful producer Joe Roth likewise shepherded *Alice in Wonderland,* and he knew that Robert would be a key component in creating the Land of Oz. "Designing fairy-tale movies is quite different than doing a movie with practical sets and existing locations," states Roth. "These are largely virtual worlds with thousands of visual effects. The computer-generated world has to mesh with physical sets and other variables. There are very few individuals who have enough experience in both worlds to make sure you're not creating two separate looks, and Robert is one of them."

With the knowledge of Robert's impressive skill set, Roth orchestrated a meeting on June 25, 2010, between director Sam Raimi and Stromberg to discuss the possibilities of working together. "I had never met Sam before, and I was a little timid at first—I was a big fan," recalls Stromberg. "But I soon realized that he's got this great heart. I already respected him as a director, as a visionary, and on top of that he's so friendly, so welcoming. We started bouncing ideas off of each other and we became very excited about doing the project." Remembering that day, Raimi says, "Robert described his vision of the world and that is the path I've been following ever since."

That path did necessitate a conversation, one that would be ongoing, about how to approach a world that had been introduced before, either through Baum's books and Denslow's illustrations, or the various other movies and stage plays that had emerged from Baum's brainchild over the years. "We couldn't copy what had been done before, and didn't want to," declares Stromberg. "We had to come up with ways to respect the fans, while attracting a new generation of devotees to the world of Oz. I scoured Baum's descriptions of the world, and I looked at all of Denslow's artwork. I wanted the influence from the books coupled with a new and unique vision that I would want to pay money to become immersed in."

AN ILLUSTRATION of Oz in his balloon by W. W. Denslow. Denslow's illustrations were one of the inspirations for the look of the film.

ENTERING THE LAND OF OZ

For Robert, immersion meant fashioning the Land of Oz from the tiniest blade of grass to the most expansive mountain range. And so, in early September 2010, Raimi, Stromberg, and a small design crew (consisting of supervising art directors Stefan Dechant and Todd Cherniawsky, both *Alice in Wonderland* and *Avatar* veterans; illustrators Jonathan Bach, Victor Martinez, Dylan Cole, Steven Messing, and Dawn Brown; set designer Tex Kadonaga; and researcher Pierre Bunikiewicz) spent the next six months in the *Oz The Great and Powerful* production offices at Tribeca West in Los Angeles. Their collaboration would ultimately form the creative foundation from which the Land of Oz would emerge.

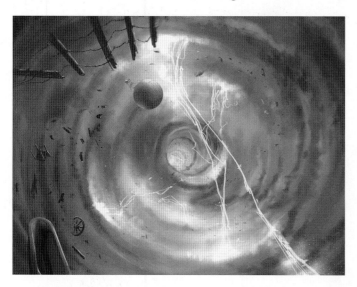

Reflecting on this period of design, executive producer Philip Steuer, himself no stranger to the task of world creation, having produced The Chronicles of Narnia films, comments, "The process of designing Oz was an ongoing, organic exploration, especially in the beginning. It was fascinating to watch. Sam, Robert, and the art department were constantly sketching out ideas, illustrating landscapes, and designing creatures. I'd walk into the art department for a meeting and see these incredible key frames from the script that I thought were the best I'd ever seen, and then I'd come in the next day and that illustration had been taken down and replaced with one that was even more mind-blowing. The unique world that was emerging was inspiring, but the speed at which that world was evolving was absolutely astounding."

(TOP) PRODUCTION DESIGNER
Robert Stromberg. Photograph by Merie Wallace.

(BOTTOM LEFT) An early illustration by Jonathan Bach shows a concept for the twister.

A BLACK AND WHITE
STUDY from inside the
twister by Victor Martinez.

A DIGITAL PAINTING by Dylan
Cole shows Oz's balloon being
carried away by a Kansas storm.

"The early stages of world creation is the period in which you get to express the most; you experiment the most," notes Stromberg. "A lot of the creative gems that emerge from these initial meetings are what you see in the final movie." One creative gem from this period not only stood the test of time, but also became the jumping-off point from which the entire world of Oz would take shape. In their inaugural meeting, Raimi and Stromberg discussed how important the first glimpse of the Land of Oz needed to be. "The world of Oz as L. Frank Baum created it has so many different countries and lands and seas and impassable mountains," states Raimi. "It's gigantic in scale, and we knew that the first time we saw this fantastic land we had to wow the audience. Robert and I challenged each other to come up with a visual that encapsulated not only the scope of Baum's imagination, but also the world of Oz that we wanted to visit."

Raimi's challenge ruminated in Stromberg's creative conscious and soon a conceptual methodology took shape. "When we first see the Land of Oz I wanted this gnarled, sort of barbed wire look. I felt Oz needed to go through some kind of a barrier to gain entry into Oz. At this juncture in the story, Oscar Diggs is escaping a somewhat troubled past and embarking upon a new chapter in his life—I wanted the visual to reflect that transition. I discussed this approach with Sam and showed him the illustration I was working on of Oz's balloon navigating these contorted rock formations with the Land of Oz in the distance. Sam studied the painting, looked at me and he said, 'That's it!'"

This eureka moment for Raimi and Stromberg was followed by a simple gesture that would, from that day forward, inspire the design of the entire film. Robert asked art department coordinator Lindsay Good to print out a six-foot-by-four-foot version of the illustration, and Good turned to trusted Los Angeles printer Ford Graphics. The next day an oversized version of Oscar Diggs' balloon floating into a new and mysterious world arrived, was unfurled, and hung on the wall inside the doorway to the art department.

Commenting on the signficance of this gesture, supervising art director Stefan Dechant states: "Robert and I both come from the school of thought that production design not only means you are designing the look of the film and building sets, but it also means you're designing the production. You are servicing the director, the cast, the crew, and the studio. We needed a visual that established a tone, a level of artistry, and commitment to the story so that no matter who walked in—actors, Disney executives, the writers—you had an instant frame of reference of the land that was being created within our walls. We put that illustration front and center, and in a lot of ways it set the tone for the entire process. People were excited when they came into the art department because of that image. They knew they were leaving one world behind and entering a new one in order to execute a vision that had never been seen before."

THIS EARLY DIGITAL
PAINTING by Production
Designer Robert Stromberg
became the capstone image as
it perfectly captured the tone
of the world the team was
bringing to life.

KANSAS

With the visual Oz is greeted with as he embarks on his incredible journey firmly in place, Raimi, Stromberg, and team did a little backtracking and discussed the world Oscar would be leaving behind. In his books, Baum described Oz as a sleight of hand performer prior to being whisked away by a current of air to the Emerald City. Expounding upon Baum's description for the purposes of his screenplay, screenwriter Mitchell Kapner detailed the surroundings we first find Oz in as follows:

KANSAS SET for *Oz*
The Great and Powerful.
Photograph by Merie Wallace.

FADE IN:

EXT. KANSAS PRAIRIE—EARLY EVENING

A gray land under a gray sky—everything flat, drab, dreary. A ramshackle farmhouse—a creaky weather vane—a dirt road stretches to nowhere—but then we see, up ahead, looming over the horizon: A LARGE LIGHTER-THAN-AIR BALLOON—below which we find:

EXT. THE BAUM & BARLEY BROS. CIRCUS

Not exactly the *Greatest Show On Earth*, but still a pretty big deal around here. People have come from far and wide—their modes of transport and their styles of dress telling us we're in the very early 1900s.

Townsfolk and farmers stroll the midway . . . barkers shout their come-ons . . . a Bearded Lady preens . . . the crowd oohs and aahs at the Daring Young Men On The Flying Trapeze . . . there's a Mangy Menagerie of elephants and monkeys and a lion.

The creative duo of Raimi and Stromberg embraced Kapner's Kansas description, but vacillated to a degree about how successful, or not, the traveling circus Oz performs in should appear. Early drawings embraced Kapner's description and further enhanced the circus' success. These illustrations housed a vibrant spectacle with a crowded midway and, rather than a "mangy menagerie," this circus had energetic giraffes, elephants, and many other exotic animals that performed in grand and colorful tents.

However, the more Raimi delved into the character of Oz—a man longing for something greater who believes his current circumstances are beneath him—the more the visuals being created conflicted with the narrative. As a result, Raimi and Stromberg embraced a starker, bleaker vision of Kansas; one that would eventually make up the opening frame of the movie.

(THIS PAGE) Kansas circus illustrations by Jonathan Bach.

BLACK AND WHITE Kansas
illustration by Robert Stromberg.

(TOP LEFT) Iconic magician Lance Burton discusses options for Oz's magic act as James Franco, Sam Raimi, and Robert Stromberg look on.

(BOTTOM AND TOP RIGHT) Concept graphics for some of the signage featured in Kansas by Ellen Lampl.

"We realized the Kansas circus needed to be more of a low-budget traveling show," says Stromberg. "Things needed to be threadbare, not pristine. This new approach added a dimensionality I'm really happy with because it reflects Oz's character in so many ways. It's also a great contrast between what he tangibly has in Kansas and the world that greets him upon arriving in Oz."

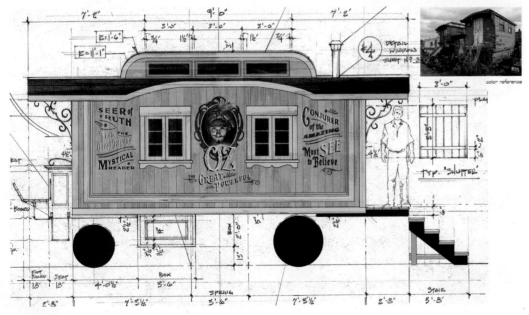

(TOP) Set photographs from the interior of Oz's trailer taken by Art Director John Lord Booth III.

(LEFT) A plan of Oz's trailer featuring reference photographs for the specific green to be used. Plan by Ellen Lampl.

ILLUSTRATION OF OZ
running through the circus
boardwalk by Jonathan Bach.

BLACK AND WHITE
Kansas illustration by
Victor Martinez.

As the creative approaches toward Kansas and the Land of Oz advanced, conversations began to be peppered with musings of how to differentiate the two even further—the bleak Kansas dust bowl Oz vacates versus the land of vibrant color, creatures, and landscapes he finds himself in. The more Sam and Robert looked at the illustrations of Kansas and compared them to the iconic painting that escorted visitors into the art department, the more an artistic plan of attack materialized. "We wanted Oz to be a fantastic and magical place for the audience," states Raimi. "So we thought Kansas should be black and white and shot in a 1.33:1 format (vintage television standard), so that we could really open up the screen to our 2.39:1 aspect ratio (wide-screen cinema standard) and dial in the color when we arrive in the Land of Oz."

To further accentuate the two worlds, Raimi decided the sound design should be altered, going from mono (one speaker) to surround sound during the transition. Additionally, he realized they could deploy the use of yet another tool in their creative arsenal—3-D. This option could be kept to a minimum in Kansas, and then fully realized while crossing into Oz to further intertwine the audience's audiovisual experience with Oscar Diggs' physical journey.

Although the world of Oz was just starting to take shape, the time was at hand to contemplate how the Land of Oz would be physically created, or not. Stromberg in particular was able to weigh in on this quandary as he had designed a film, *Alice in Wonderland,* that, for the most part built relatively few practical sets or props and instead opted for a computer-generated world. "The approach we took on *Alice* was spot-on for that film," says Robert. "The look we wanted and the methodology we used to achieve it worked in tandem. In the case of *Oz The Great and Powerful,* there was a solid reason why I pitched that we should build sets on soundstages and have a mix of practical and CGI sets. There's a certain artifice that we all were going for in general—almost a theatrical stagelike quality. If we were to go out and build a Yellow Brick Road on a hillside in Ireland, it wouldn't have that feeling. I don't think you can get that from completely digital worlds either. So the only way to achieve our vision was to build large sets on soundstages and extend those in the computer. We decided to use visual effects in a supportive role rather than a role that takes over all aspects of filmmaking."

In Raimi, Stromberg found a supportive voice for this approach. "It was important for me to have a lot of sets for the actors," states Sam. "I really wanted them to have something to touch—something to see and interact with that could inform their performance. And, it's not just the actors who benefit and are informed by tangible sets and props. I wanted practical elements to likewise inform the CGI artists in postproduction. If there is something practical in the frame, the artists are able to take over a shot with a very clear understanding of what it is that we are going for—dappled sunlight raking across the actors, textures of bricks, the color of an Emerald City wall, and those sorts of things. They're able to do a continuation of what we've established on set with an informed frame of reference."

OVERHEAD VIEW of the Kansas circus set on Stage 1 of the Michigan Motion Picture Studios in Pontiac, Michigan. Photograph by John Lord Booth III.

One would be hard-pressed to find two filmmakers more qualified than Raimi and Stromberg to formulate, present and execute a creative blueprint as to how best achieve their collective vision. With Raimi's Spider-Man experience combining practical sets and locations with an ample mix of animated characters and CG set extensions, coupled with Stromberg's expertise with similar elements from *Alice in Wonderland* and *Avatar*, the executives at Disney urged the team to proceed. Perhaps Stromberg best summed up the resolution when he said, "I would have been more frightened by this decision if I didn't have a couple of big mountains in the rearview mirror."

(**TOP**) An example of how the production mixed both practical sets with digital set and landscape extensions. Photograph by Merie Wallace.

(**BOTTOM**) Oz's trailer elevated for a shot looking up through a trapdoor. Photograph by John Lord Booth III.

THE **WHIMSIE WOODS**

With a key *Oz The Great and Powerful* visual in place, the general look of Kansas on paper, and an overall practical design methodology decided upon, Stromberg and company embarked upon imagining the rest of the world. Before doing so, however, Stromberg went back to the creative well that had such an impact on him as a child. "I wanted to look again at the early Disney designs that influenced me as a kid," relates Stromberg. "I called the powers-that-be at Disney, and they arranged for me to get a tour of their archives, where a lot of the originals still exist. I looked at the old illustrations—*Snow White and the Seven Dwarfs, Bambi, Pinocchio*—and I realized how much I wanted to expand upon them. Not only did I admire the artwork, but also I wanted to take that classic approach and make it photo-real with today's visual effects techniques. It was clear that I could harvest these older ideas, make something that we've never seen before, while still retaining that classic Disney essence."

In addition to the Mouse House masterpieces, there were five other instrumental spheres of influence that Robert and the art department turned to for inspiration: the Hudson River School (the name given to a group of New York City-based landscape painters that rose to prominence around 1850 and focused on idealized naturalism marked by dramatic forms and vigorous technique); Grant Wood (an American painter best known for his work depicting rural America); Art Nouveau (the early twentieth century style introduced into European art and architecture distinguished by its use of curved lines, patterns, and a return to natural elements such as plants and flowers); Art Deco (an eclectic artistic and design style recognized by its linear symmetry, and functionality); and Stromberg's own imagination. "In the early stages of designing a film, I get inspired by what I want to see; by worlds I want to visit," he says. "I need it to be fun for myself, and then I want it to be exciting for the people who decide to go on this journey with us."

ARTWORK from *Bambi* (this page) and *Snow White and the Seven Dwarfs* (opposite page) depict the inspiration behind many of Stromberg's designs, particularly the trees in the Whimsie Woods.

The first territory in Oz that needed inspiration was that of the Whimsies. Specifically, the script called for two sets that would become known as the Whimsie Riverbank, and the Whimsie Woods. Fans of Baum's adventures know the Whimsies to be an aggressive, simple minded race prone to wearing masks to hide their grotesquely misshapen heads. While Baum was quite descriptive about the Whimsies from the neck up, precious little was written about the land in which they lived.

With little to go on from Baum, there was a key component in the overall narrative that provided guidance. After navigating the barbed, rocky peaks, this was the terra firma Oz first steps upon after his balloon crash-lands; it was Oz's first up close interaction with the new world. Therefore, Sam and Robert wanted the surroundings to be like nothing Oz had ever seen before. He had to be in a world beyond even his wildest dreams. "I wanted the land of the Whimsies to have a real storybook quality to them with lush, oversized plants and flowers," notes Stromberg. "These were two of the sets I drew heavy inspiration on from Disney. I knew that I wanted trees to be a visual anchor and I immediately thought of the trees in *Snow White and the Seven Dwarfs*. I asked myself, 'If I made them photo-real, what would they look like?'"

OZ'S BALLOON lands on
the bank of the Whimsie
Woods in this early painting
by Robert Stromberg.

DIGITAL PAINTING
by Robert Stromberg and
Michelle Moen.

(THIS PAGE) Early tree concept designs by, clockwise from the top, Jonathan Bach, Victor Martinez, and Daphne Yap.

(OPPOSITE PAGE) Whimsie Woods illustrations by Robert Stromberg.

To answer this question, Stromberg started with a pencil sketch, scanned the drawing of the Disney-esque tree into Photoshop, and then began adding layers of detail. Commenting on this approach, which is commonplace for Robert, he states, "In a lot of ways, my background in matte painting really comes into play. In the old days, we'd do a photo-real painting on glass or amazonite, and then combine that in camera with the live-action element, making one shot. That's still what I'm doing, but with digital technology. I'll take an element that I know is going to be real—in this case the tree—and then start using some of the old-school painting techniques to add photo-real layers around it until what I see in my head is on the screen."

OZ TREES

DAPHNE YAP

OZ

Interestingly, as the world of the Whimsies progressed toward completion, the Whimsies themselves receded into the background, and then were omitted altogether. The decision to remove the Whimsies was twofold: they were an expensive design element, particularly for the costume department, but more importantly, they didn't progress the narrative. Storywise, the Whimsie Riverbank and Woods exist to introduce Oz to this fantastical new world, and to provide the backdrop on which Oz meets Theodora. Therefore, the cranially challenged warriors were an interesting visual, but not a necessary one.

There was a component to the Whimsie Woods that became increasingly necessary as design conversations between Raimi and Stromberg progressed. "I was looking at the lushness of the Whimsie Woods in the illustrations and the incredible details contained within—the plants and flowers of all sizes and colors, the moss on the trees, the various grasses—and I knew that we were going to need the best greens coordinators in the business to pull off Sam and Rob's vision. For me, that's Dan Gillooly and Richard Bell," states Dechant. "Luckily we got them both, and looking back, I can't overstate their contribution to the picture. I don't think we could have done it without them. Their work was amazing and really brought the sets to life, literally."

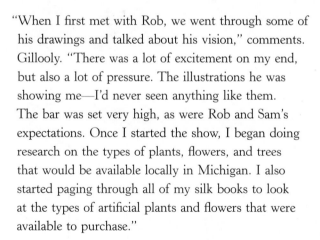

"When I first met with Rob, we went through some of his drawings and talked about his vision," comments. Gillooly. "There was a lot of excitement on my end, but also a lot of pressure. The illustrations he was showing me—I'd never seen anything like them. The bar was set very high, as were Rob and Sam's expectations. Once I started the show, I began doing research on the types of plants, flowers, and trees that would be available locally in Michigan. I also started paging through all of my silk books to look at the types of artificial plants and flowers that were available to purchase."

(OPPOSITE PAGE) Dan Gillooly and Robert Loring on the Whimsie Woods set. Photograph by John Lord Booth III.

(TOP LEFT) Whimsie Woods tree study by Jonathan Bach.

(TOP) Richard Bell (right) and Andrew Jones (left) on the Whimsie Woods set.

(MIDDLE) Flying fish concept art by Steven Qi Jin. The flying fish are inhabitants of the Whimsie River.

(BOTTOM) Whimsie Woods painting by Dylan Cole.

The more research Gillooly did on Michigan flora as compared to the bold art department depictions of the Whimsie Woods, the more apparent it became that it was going to take a healthy combination of artificial silk flowers and organic flowers and plants. "I worked with Rob on *Alice* and we got to be comfortable around each other. He was impressed that my crew and I could creatively take the ball and run with it without a whole lot of direction," says Gillooly. "And that is one of the things we had to do on *Oz the Great and Powerful*. Initially it was challenging because we didn't exactly know how everything was going to come together, but we started playing with combinations. For instance, to pull off some of the designs it was evident that I needed plants with larger leaves and stems to visually support these enormous flowers. So I ordered tropical plants from Florida and had them sent to Michigan. I also brought in a massive bunch of large leaf philodendrons and elephant ears. Everything ended up blending perfectly. Once we got past those initial questions, we got comfortable with the overall approach and things really progressed. Rob would come in and see some of the combinations we were working on. He'd have this big smile on his face and say, 'Yeah, now we're going somewhere.' That's when we knew we were taking it to a different level."

SAM RAIMI AND JAMES FRANCO rehearse on the Whimsie Riverbank set. Photograph by Merie Wallace.

(TOP) Whimsie Woods landscape by Victor Martinez.

(MIDDLE) A photograph by John Lord Booth III showing the detail within the Whimsie Woods set.

(BOTTOM) Whimsie Woods fauna scale chart by Daphne Yap.

Oz Plants Line Up

6'

1   2   3   4   5   6

(TOP) Early illustrations by Jonathan Bach that led to the ultimate creation of the Whimsie Riverbank.

(BOTTOM) Whimsie Woods set. Photograph by John Lord Booth III.

OZ AND THEODORA run through the Whimsie Woods. Paintover by Robert Stromberg.

THIS SET PHOTOGRAPH shows the elaborate detail and the level of attention used by the greens team—both with real and artificial pieces—to create the Whimsie Woods. Photograph by John Lord Booth III.

Eventually, in the Whimsie Woods, the ratio of artificial versus organic netted out at about seventy-five/twenty-five. For the rest of the sets, the ratio was approximately fifty/fifty. "The challenge with real flowers is that they don't last long on a stage—they change. They grow, they bloom, they wilt, and they die," comments Gillooly. "Not only do we need the sets to remain really colorful, but for continuity, they have to look the same."

Gillooly and Bell were able to begin a portion of the Whimsie Woods creative process in Los Angeles, but it was not until their boots were on the ground in Michigan that one of the key components of the Whimsie Woods fell into place—the trees from *Snow White and the Seven Dwarfs* that Robert Stromberg wanted to make photo-real. "We knew we had to get the trees right. They were the biggest part of the Whimsie Woods set, and once again we knew we were going to be combining the artificial with the organic in order to pull off Stromberg's unique vision," states Gillooly.

In addition to Gillooly and Bell, it would take a small army of craftsmen to actualize Stromberg's tribute to Walt Disney's trees. The process began with the overall silhouette of the tree being crafted out of massive foam blocks. As this was being realized, construction coordinator Jeff Passanante's team methodically welded a steel armature that created the "skeleton" of the tree. Once finalized,

the silhouette was fashioned around the armature and the sculptors further accentuated the shapes of the trunk and limbs. Upon completion, a section of PVC pipe was joined to the end of each limb. Plasterers then added layer after layer of plaster, meticulously adding vein work to the trees in order to give the look of grain and bark. Once the plaster dried, painters descended upon the work of art and applied the finishing touches to make it look like a tree.

However, the trees were not photo-real until the greensmen got their hands on them to add the moss, limbs, and surrounding ferns. Gillooly and Bell's participation with the moss and the ferns was easy to understand, but a question that was raised by many a visitor staring at a nub-covered tree was: "Why not go ahead and sculpt the tree limbs as well? Why the need for practical tree limbs?"

The answer to that inquiry lay in a theme that presented itself not only in the script, but also in the strategy the art department enacted to design the entire film as fiscally responsible as possible. The narrative was full of contrasts. The lush Whimsie Woods contrasted with that of the dead, decrepit Dark Forest. The masculine, green, Art Deco-inspired Emerald City was in contrast to the feminine, earth tones of the Art Nouveau-inspired Glinda's kingdom.

PAGES 80–83 represent the progression of a Whimsie tree from model to final set piece. Photographs by John Lord Booth III.

To exploit these narrative contrasts, the art department realized early on that this also presented an opportunity to create "sister sets" where a large portion of an existing set could be repurposed to create the building blocks of another. Not only was this beneficial financially, but it was also creatively advantageous. A visual familiarity could be established in one scene, and then revisited in another, contrasting set. The audience knows, consciously or not, that the two are linked together. Expounding upon this technique, Stromberg remarks: "I've always been a believer that the environment dictates what the mood is at any given moment. In our film I've tried to pay attention to what's happening in the story line so that the environments are appropriate. It may not be something the audience picks up immediately, but it's important over time when you're watching a movie. You don't understand why you feel a certain way, but you do because there is a built-in tone and familiarity with the environment."

"When you watch the film," explains Dechant, "it's no coincidence that Oz and Theodora run down a knoll in the Whimsie Woods and hide under a cave within an overhang that knoll creates. After the threat they are running from passes, they emerge and continue out onto a flat portion of the woods. Conversely, later on, when Oz enters the Dark Forest with Finley and China Girl in tow, they walk along a flat portion of the Yellow Brick Road and the scene ends with them traversing a hill to a grave site. The two locations are essentially the same set, but flipped and redressed. Financially you only build the 'bones' one time, and creatively Sam and Rob are able to establish familiarity to set up subtle dichotomies—good versus evil, light versus dark." As a result of the sets doing double-duty, certain portions of the designs, the trees in particular, had to pull a double shift as well. The most efficient way to convert a lively, lush tree into a dead, brittle one was to replace the limbs, thus the need for the PVC infused into the tree's design. The pipe naturally housed a hole at the end into which a vibrant limb could be inserted or easily removed and replaced with a dead one.

Commenting on this process and the hunt for the perfect limbs, Gillooly recalls: "Apple tree limbs in particular have incredible character—a lot of swoops and bends. Specifically, apple trees in orchards because they are pruned back and after awhile they're almost like bonsai trees. Their limbs get thick and they start taking weird turns. I must have walked through half a dozen apple orchards looking for the right limbs. Most people thought I was nuts and we weren't having much luck until we met a guy whose orchard hadn't been in operation for a while. He showed us around and his limbs were amazing. We harvested all of our stuff there, hauled them in, and inserted the apple tree limbs into the sculpts—perfect."

The trees complete, Gillooly and Bell spent another six weeks bringing the Whimsie Woods set to life, literally. "With so much dirt and grass and plants and flowers, coupled with the amount of watering we had to do to keep everything alive, you inevitably end up creating a mini-ecosystem," observes Gillooly. "We had creatures scurrying about inside Stage 2, birds flying around, resting in the trees. And then there were the crickets. The crickets ended up being a real challenge for sound."

WHIMSIE WOODS illustration
by Robert Stromberg.

THE **DARK FOREST**

Thankfully for the sound department, Sam and the crew achieved all the shots needed in the Whimsie Woods and the production was able to progress to Stromberg's design for the next set on the docket: the Dark Forest.

With its sinister trees, dead brambles, and an overwhelming thirst for water, the design was not as critter-friendly as the Whimsie Woods. However, it too was inspired by past Disney iconic elements such as the previously designed iconic trees from *Snow White and the Seven Dwarfs*. From there, Robert let his imagination run wild. "The Dark Forest is pure Rob," states Dechant. "He knew exactly how he wanted that world to look, the trees in particular, to the point that we built miniatures of them in Los Angeles so that by the time we arrived in Detroit there was a very specific visual that couldn't be misinterpreted."

A **PHOTOGRAPH** of the brambles
used in the Dark Forest.
Photograph by Scott Stokdyk.

When it came time to see Stromberg's vision come to fruition at Michigan Motion Picture Studios, as with the Whimsie Woods, Gillooly and Bell were called in to complete the vision. "The Dark Forest was a 180 degree creative turn for us. It was built on top of the repurposed Whimsie Woods set, so the first thing we had to do was take out everything green. The iconic trees themselves were part of both sets, so we had to take all the limbs out and replace them with their dead counterpart," recalls Gillooly.

(TOP) The creepy forest in *Snow White and the Seven Dwarfs* was one of many sources of inspiration behind Stromberg's designs.

(BOTTOM) An early Dark Forest tree sketch by Victor Martinez.

Ironically, when it came time to secure the ideal replacement limbs for the trees in the Dark Forest, a contrasting sister orchard to the one where the apple limbs had been harvested presented itself. "The owner of the apple orchard also had a peach orchard nearby that had died," states Gillooly. "He mentioned that the first time I was there and I kept this in the back of my mind. When it came time to create the Dark Forest, I went knocking on his door again, and sure enough, the dead peach limbs were exactly what we were looking for."

(TOP) A still from *Snow White and the Seven Dwarfs* shows the beloved Disney classic's influence in creating the Dark Forest.

(BOTTOM) A digital painting by Robert Stromberg of the forest.

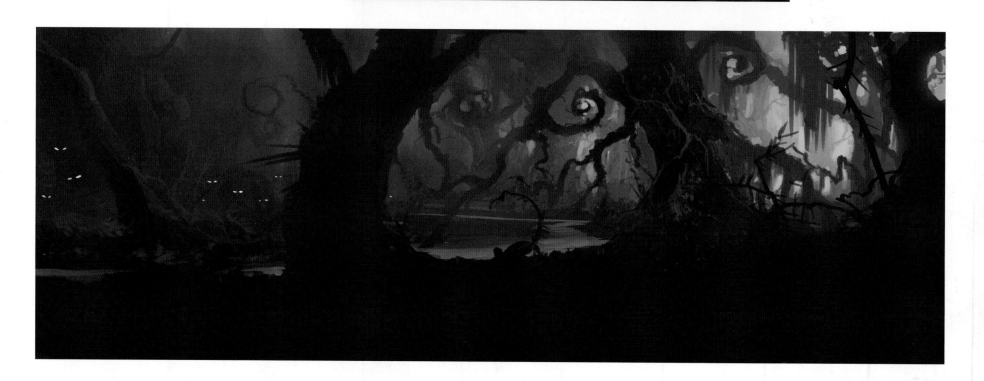

(TOP) Dark Forest digital painting by Robert Stromberg.

(BOTTOM) Dark Forest tree studies by Jonathan Bach.

There was an additional design element to Stromberg's Dark Forest that Gillooly had kept in the back of his mind; the briar patch that he had seen in early illustrations while prepping in Los Angeles. While driving to work one day in Detroit, Gillooly passed by a field full of thistle that he knew would be perfect to accentuate the design. When it was time to dress the Dark Forest, the greens team descended upon the field and harvested the thistles. Following Stromberg's direction, they took the thistles, dead leaves, brambles, and a new element, grape vines, and started dressing in the set. "We began playing around with the grape vines, doing big loops, and it really brought the design to life," comments Gillooly. "We then added some four-inch thorns that we fabricated and glued to the vines. The result was these huge, really threatening briar patches. Stromberg loved it."

"The Dark Forest is the only place in Oz that feels really dangerous," says art director John Lord Booth III. "The forest is supposed to feel like a place that Evanora and Theodora forgot. Nobody wants to go there. It had to feel scary and it had to feel dead. That's the tone that Stromberg's illustrations set, and that's what Dan Gillooly and Richie Bell were able to help pull off."

(THIS PAGE) Set photographs of the cemetery within the Dark Forest. Photographs by Merie Wallace.

DIGITAL PAINTING of the
cemetery set by Victor Martinez.

DIGITAL PAINTING of a
precipice within the Whimsie
Woods by Robert Stromberg.

THE EMERALD CITY

In addition to the Whimsie Woods and the Dark Forest, which were on the outskirts of Ozian civilizations, Stromberg and his creative team were likewise designing two epic cities that were central to the story line of *Oz The Great and Powerful:* the Emerald City and Glinda's kingdom. Naturally, the look of these two urban settings would differ greatly from their rural counterparts, but there was a design theme that remained—contrasts. Specifically, the contrasting artistic styles were the Art Deco-infused domain of Evanora and Theodora, the Emerald City, and the Art Nouveau-inspired world of Glinda's kingdom.

To keep these contrasting styles the driving forces behind their respective designs, the two worlds were purposefully envisioned in tandem. Commenting on the differing approaches, Stromberg states: "In regard to the colors and textures used in the movie, I decided early on that I wanted Emerald City to be a very masculine place with strong, hard lines. As a result, Art Deco became the driving inspiration. On the other hand, in Glinda's world I wanted a much more feminine quality, more curves. So I chose Art Nouveau to inform the classic Disney castle motif we chose for her kingdom."

THIS IMAGE by Jonathan Bach illustrates an idea for a look for the Emerald City Square during the day.

In regard to the Emerald City, there was also a story point Raimi and Stromberg wanted to hint at, and Art Deco helped set their desired tone. "Sam and Rob wanted the Emerald City to have a masculine impression in order to make it feel as if the kingdom was not a by-product of the sisters," remarks Dechant. "The throne wasn't made for them, it was made for the king. Art Deco created that male ambiance."

(THIS PAGE) Early digital painting of Glinda's Kingdom by Robert Stromberg and Dylan Cole.

(OPPOSITE PAGE) The Emerald City looms above the viewer in this piece by Dylan Cole.

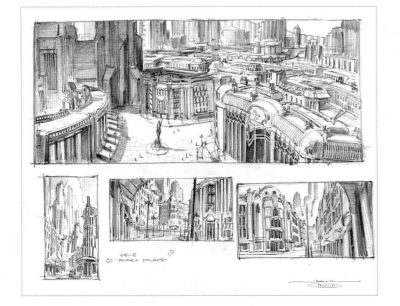

ILLUSTRATOR Jonathan Bach's pencil sketch studies for the Emerald City streets.

(TOP LEFT) A carriage study by Jonathan Bach.

(TOP RIGHT) Emerald City carriage illustration by Michelle Moen and Tex Kadonaga.

(BOTTOM) Evanora sends forth her baboons in this painting by Jonathan Bach.

CONCEPT WORK by Jonathan Bach
(top) and Iain McFadyen (bottom left),
alongside marble samples that were
used to develop and create the Throne
Room's final finish (bottom right).

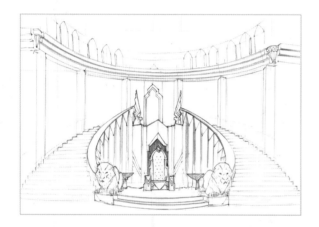

With the overall Art Deco blueprint in place, one set in particular became a creative launchpad from which the rest of the city was created, the Throne Room. "The Emerald City Throne Room is where Oz meets Evanora for the first time," comments Stromberg. "For her introduction, I wanted this real old-Hollywood moment. She comes down the stairway in a long dress, and I envisioned a cascading stairway, something like you might see in a Busby Berkeley musical, to accentuate her character. This set is definitely a tribute to those films of the 1930s and '40s. I don't think I would have been able to pull it off if I wasn't influenced by the films of that era as a young person."

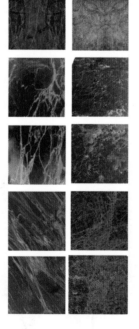

Commenting on another influence, as well as the overall design intent, Dechant states: "It's very much like the Barbara Stanwyck reveal in *Double Indemnity*. When Walter Neff (Fred MacMurray) comes in and sees Phyllis (Stanwyck), she's in this sexy position of power. That's what drove the Throne Room design. Sam and Rob really wanted that powerful reveal. And, when you couple that with the narrative requirements, things really started to fall into place. The first thing you needed to see was the throne, so that Oz could have that covetous moment. But the next thing that needs to draw the eye is Evanora, because she's the keeper of said throne; she's in the position of power. That's why we had those stairs, which are slightly unconventional. They frame the throne and, almost like an arrow, point up to Evanora. An additional strategic design piece was the window behind her. By placing it there, she could be backlit and in silhouette. She then steps into the light, making her reveal as dramatic as possible."

The Art Deco Throne Room design was moving full steam ahead and it was now time to decide upon the shade of green that would embody the iconic city. To aid in this process, Stromberg called upon the services of veteran paint supervisor Tom Brown. "In our initial meeting," recalls Brown, "Rob and I started by looking at gems—green onyx, emeralds, etc. It was through the careful study of these natural elements that we found our green, which was a hybrid of these gems."

"The importance of finding the right green is obvious when designing the Emerald City, but it was such an integral moment because it affected so many other areas," recollects Dechant. "Sam wanted the green to 'read,' meaning he needed the same green to be able to portray a variety of moods. When Oscar Diggs first arrives at the Emerald City, he wanted the green to have an inviting feel. Later on in the story, he wanted those same sets, those same greens, to emanate a more ominous impression. This went on to affect how Peter lit the sets, as well as the green Gary Jones and Michael Kutsche used in the costumes. It was an important outcome and a lot of departments were able to build upon that decision."

STROMBERG'S CONCEPT for the Throne Room (top) compared to the set itself (bottom right, photograph by Merie Wallace) and in a final shot from the film (bottom left).

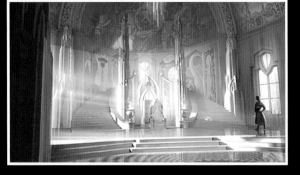
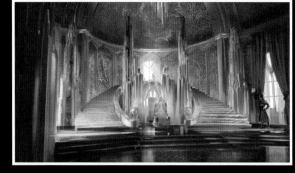

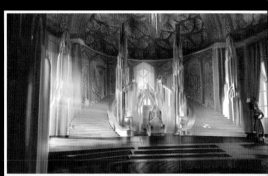

(THESE PAGES) Early interior
Throne Room lighting studies by
Jonathan Bach.

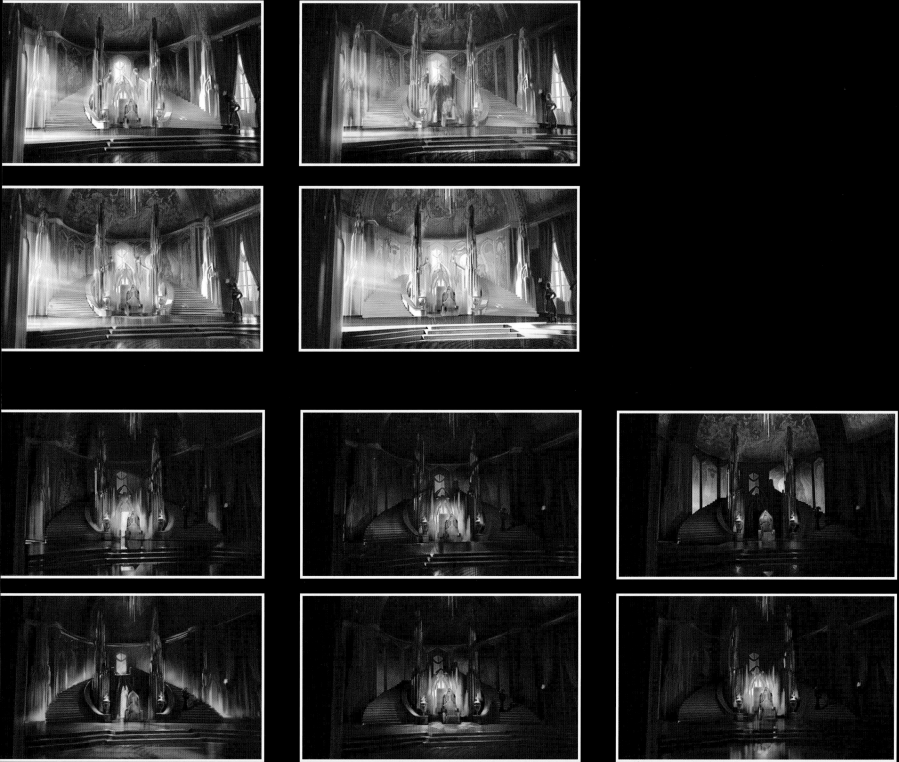

AN EARLY ITERATION of Glinda's castle by Victor Martinez.

GLINDA'S KINGDOM

As the Emerald City was being envisioned with straight edges and right angles, Stromberg was likewise entrenched in the design of Glinda's Art Nouveau-inspired kingdom, highlighted by natural structures and curved lines. "Glinda's kingdom, particularly her castle, is a mixture of a variety of elements," states Stromberg. "It has an Art Nouveau quality to it, but I also wanted that classic Disney castle look infused with elements from the Gardens of Babylon. Narratively, I chose these elements because I really wanted to create a contrast between her world and that of the rival witches."

(THIS PAGE) A sketch of Glinda's castle by Jonathan Bach.

(OPPOSITE PAGE) As the Art Nouveau inspiration was embraced, the look of Glinda's castle transformed accordingly in this digital painting by Dylan Cole.

As with most of the designs for *Oz The Great and Powerful*, the process of illustrating Glinda's castle began with a napkin sketch from Stromberg that was a clear homage to the Disney castle featured in their logo. From there, a lot of research was done on stone buildings that featured the deceptively intricate Art Nouveau style. "Nouveau is tough,"

comments Dechant. "There's such a subtlety to it. It's not just inserting a lot of curves and flowers into a design. We did a lot of research on Alphonse Mucha and especially Hector Guimard. We studied Guimard for his exteriors, particularly his work on the Agar Apartments in Paris, because we were creating a castle with intricate stonework."

Working with stone and Art Nouveau accoutrements was key to the look of Glinda's kingdom, but it was a design element inspired by Glinda's mode of transportation that tied her world together thematically. "Glinda travels by bubble," expounds Stromberg. "That's pretty iconic, and I wanted to incorporate a bubble theme into her character, into her world. I like to look at sets as what the actor is wearing to a degree. To me that is very important in dictating what the mood should be and how comfortable the character is in their environment. So we started to look at the castle walls. At first it was just going to be classic stone. But I wanted to see if there was a way that if the light hit it just right, a certain iridescent sheen with a rainbow pattern could emerge."

EARLY PENCIL and painted examples of Glinda's castle, executed by Jonathan Bach.

GLINDA'S CASTLE seems to float above the land in this breathtaking digital painting by Robert Stromberg.

(THIS PAGE) Glinda's courtyard. Note the signature luminescence on the castle walls reacting to the light. Photograph by Merie Wallace.

(OPPOSITE PAGE) An interior shot of Glinda's library, where the Art Nouveau inspiration is readily apparent. Photograph by Merie Wallace.

Robert's bubble motif for Glinda's kingdom was embraced throughout the various departments. If you study Glinda's dress you'll find a pearlescent quality to it when the light hits it just right. Likewise, when you walk around Glinda's library and you study set decorator Nancy Haigh's wallpaper, the slag shades for the lamps, and her choice of Fabergé eggs, an iridescent sheen emerges as the light finds the different objects. However, the one department that had the biggest challenge instituting the bubble theme—paint supervisor Tom Brown and his team—was the one directly responsible for realizing Stromberg's initial inspiration. "Initially, Glinda's castle was just stone," comments Brown. "And then Rob introduced the bubble idea, which was genius, but it was challenging and time-consuming. We played with that for weeks. It was like painting with light. We'd get our pearlescent and iridescent washes the right transparency, and then move the light over it only to find it didn't match the section we just completed. Remaining consistent was the real challenge because the set varied—it had curves, straight lines, walls, stairs, areas that were shadowed; the light interacted with each surface in a different manner."

Supervising art director Todd Cherniawsky elaborates on the challenge: "There's such a difference working with a four-by-four-foot proof of concept piece, as compared to an entire set that has thirty-foot walls. You can very easily get misled as to how much it's going to kick when the light hits it. Tom also had the additional challenge that not only was he creating this look, he was also aging the castle. Glinda's kingdom has been around awhile. So it was a two-part process. He had to develop the new look, and then he had to knock it down so that it didn't look like a brand-new set."

1ST ASSISTANT DIRECTOR
K.C. Hodenfield stands in front of Glinda's castle steps discussing the day's work with the background actors. Photograph by Merie Wallace.

1
2
3
4
5
6
7
8

Oz Topiaries
Daphne Yap

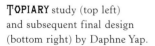

TOPIARY study (top left)
and subsequent final design
(bottom right) by Daphne Yap.

To aid in this aging process, and to embrace the
Art Nouveau inspired, bubbled-themed design,
the greens team was called in once Tom's paint
had dried. "Glinda's courtyard was really more
about enhancement of the architecture, but we
also played with the fact that Glinda traveled by
bubble," explains Gillooly. "Her world has spherical
influences and we played with that on set. There
were topiary spheres everywhere. The vines grew
into curls. Richie and his crew spent a lot of time
on that set. They were the right people and they
nailed it."

CHINA TOWN

Having grown up idolizing Walt Disney and the classic movies he made, designing, and completing Glinda's castle was a very personal process for Stromberg. However, there was another set that proved to be equally personal, if not more so, for Robert—China Town.

In his book, *The Wonderful Wizard of Oz*, Baum describes China Town as:

> *. . . a great stretch of country having a floor as smooth and shining and white as the bottom of a big platter. Scattered around were many houses made entirely of china and painted in the brightest colors. These houses were quite small, the biggest of them reaching only as high as Dorothy's waist. There were also pretty little barns, with china fences around them; and many cows and sheep and horses and pigs and chickens, all made of china, were standing about in groups.*

(THIS PAGE) The floor plan for China Girl's house by Tex Kadonaga (top), an early sketch of China Town by Warren Manser (bottom left), and a China Girl design by Michael Kutsche (bottom right).

(OPPOSITE PAGE) The China Town set that was housed on Stage 1 in Michigan Motion Picture Studios. Photograph by Merie Wallace.

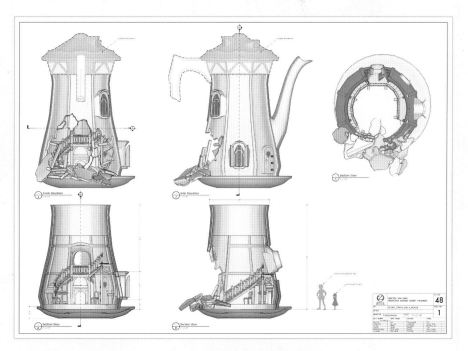

Stromberg took Baum's description into account, but as he started sketching the unusual land made of china, something else pushed its way to the forefront of his creative conscious. "I have a young daughter and I was trying to imagine what she would want to see, where she would want to play. I did something similar with the Whimsie Woods and the Dark Forest. I also have a young son and I was asking myself, 'Where would he want to play? Where would he want to be?' The more I asked myself these questions in regard to China Town, the clearer things became and this wonderful place emerged. It's almost a playhouse gone mad, and it has a scale that is somewhere between miniature and real. With that, we got the benefit of Oz feeling out of place, but I also got the benefit of working with miniatures, which I've always loved. My dad built miniatures and did miniature photography, so for a variety of reasons there's a very special place in my heart for the design of China Town and that set."

To achieve the look of Stromberg's China Town, supervising art director Todd Cherniawsky, art director Andrew Jones, and supervising painter Tom Brown had to overcome some challenges comparable to the ones they had to surmount when painting Glinda's castle. Once two of the key set pieces arrived in Pontiac (a miniature china house built by Los Angeles-based New Deal Studios and an oversized teapot on loan from Disney that was used for filming *Alice in Wonderland*), a complex question presented itself: just how much like china can China Town be?

"The choice had major implications for visual effects," elaborates Cherniawsky. "Because we were re-creating china, we had already decided to go with a Dutch white, which has a lot of blue in it. On top of that, after we saw how the light was interacting with the glazed surfaces, we had to determine just how shiny and specular it could be. I could just see Scott Stokdyk [visual effects supervisor] and Tamara Watts Kent [visual effects producer] running the other way."

THE UNIQUE and carefully crafted color of the porcelain is evident in the practical set of the tiny village.

The challenge Cherniawsky alludes to is a result of the sets being surrounded by a massive blue screen. Blue is used because it is one of the easiest colors for the computer and the digital artist to separate foreground from background, and then add the digital landscapes. Understandably, this process becomes quite difficult when the set starts to mirror the surface from which it is supposed to be extracted. Add to that the blue component the Dutch white brought to the table and the predicament becomes apparent.

"In the end, the solution for us was to add a little bit of yellow on top of the Dutch white to cut the blue," states Brown. "It took a long time to get that white balance right, while getting the glazing to a point where it could photograph as china without disrupting the VFX [visual effects] world. Director of photography Peter Deming and on-set painter Carmine Goglia deserve a lot of credit for pulling it off. That was a tough set, but it looked magical when we were done with it."

A DIGITAL PAINTING of China Town by Robert Stromberg.

OZ AND FINLEY make their way through China Town in this illustration by Matt Codd.

THE **YELLOW BRICK ROAD**

It was quite fortuitous that a yellow hue came to China Town's rescue. Because of the Yellow Brick Road, if there was any color in addition to emerald green that the *Oz The Great and Powerful* paint department had in surplus, it was yellow.

The journey toward conceptualizing the Yellow Brick Road began with a peek at Baum's books. Although it has become one of, if not the, popular culture crown jewel in the Land of Oz, Baum's descriptions of the Yellow Brick Road were quite general. Perhaps its best description comes in chapter ten of *The Patchwork Girl of Oz*:

It was a broad road, but not straight, for it wandered over hill and dale and picked out the easiest places to go. All its length and breadth was paved with smooth bricks of a bright yellow color, so it was smooth and level except in a few places where the bricks had crumbled or been removed, leaving holes that might cause the unwary to stumble.

With limited creative direction to go on from Baum, the design of the Yellow Brick Road and its surrounding bucolic landscapes truly began with a conversation between Stromberg and respected concept artist Dylan Cole. Stromberg discussed his vision of the Yellow Brick Road and the inspirations he was pulling from: the majestic scope inherent in the work of those associated with the Hudson River School and painter Grant Wood's peaceful, rolling countryside landscapes. Taking Stromberg's vision and inspirations into account, Cole went away and worked out a variety of design components he felt were key. Shortly thereafter he came back, unveiled a painting of Oz walking contemplatively along the Yellow Brick Road, and you could have heard a pin drop. Commenting on the landscape by Cole, Dechant says: "Dylan's painting is so successful because it draws you in and your eyes can't help but follow the Yellow Brick Road. And then you want to go past that area, you want to explore. You start asking yourself, 'What other lands lay ahead? What lies beyond that mountain? What lies beyond that hill?' He created a dreamscape that's all about the potential in the Land of Oz. There are two paintings paramount in the design of Oz. The first one is Stromberg's painting of Oscar Diggs' balloon entering Oz; the second is Dylan's painting of Oz walking along the Yellow Brick Road."

(OPPOSITE PAGE) Our hero pauses for a moment on the Yellow Brick Road in this digital painting by Robert Stromberg.

(THIS PAGE) Oz wanders down the Yellow Brick Road in this seminal painting by Dylan Cole.

Besides Dylan's monumental effort, the Yellow Brick Road started to appear in a variety of landscapes, and it soon became apparent that the iconic walkway had multiple personalities. As a component of the Emerald City, it was straight and pristine with clean edges. While in Glinda's kingdom, it had playful curves, and although it was cleaned just as often as its Emerald City counterpart, it had a temperament that was far more inviting and "lived in." While making its way through China Town, it became smaller, like the people and houses that lined its path. And, while creeping through the Dark Forest, the road was gnarled, root-ridden, uninviting, and forgotten like the land surrounding it.

In addition to Dylan Cole's painting and the various yellow brick personas it inspired, the design of the Yellow Brick Road had another breakthrough moment—the decision to create the road brick by singular brick. "That sounds simplistic," states Dechant, "but it was a big deal. There were other, easier techniques available to us, like using a skin that you spread over a foundation that has the yellow bricks printed on it. Or, another commonly used technique is pouring the plaster and stamping in the bricks. But from past experience we knew both of these options presented a problem. We were creating so much road, after awhile you'd pick up patterns and these techniques would expose themselves."

The conversations that led to the use of a singular brick were just the initial step that launched a battery of experiments Baum's famous creation would have to endure. There were tests to determine if the bricks should run horizontal or longitudinal. Trials to determine the thickness, color, and the amount of glaze needed were also constructed. There were studies done on the edges— should they have a rounded chamfer (a beveled edge connecting two surfaces) or a pure chamfer? And, once the chamfer was decided upon, was there a need for a camber, or a rise, in the middle of the road so that it was sloped, not flat? "We researched every brick and brick road we could think of," explains Dechant. And in the end?

"It's tile," Dechant says with a smile, "And they are about a half-inch thick. That's all we needed because that's the only portion you see. We got to where we were making five hundred 'bricks' a day."

(THIS PAGE) A sketch of the Yellow Brick Road by Warren Manser (left) compared to the realized set (right). Photograph by Melissa Franco.

(OPPOSITE PAGE) An in-process set piece for the Yellow Brick Road (left). Photograph by John Lord Booth III. Director Sam Raimi walks along the Yellow Brick Road after discussing a shot with James Franco (right). Photograph by Merie Wallace.

(TOP) An illustration of the looming Dark Forest with a gnarled Yellow Brick Road by artist Michelle Moen.

(BOTTOM) A more pristine version of the Yellow Brick Road as it leaves the Emerald City. Photograph by Melissa Franco.

As for the color of the tile, that's a little harder to pin the *Oz The Great and Powerful* art department down on. "It's a little bit of cadmium," states Cherniawsky, "but Tom has dropped it down a little bit with ambers and purples." Adds Brown with a grin, "We also weighted it by adding those glazes, because yellow can sometimes float to the surface."

(LEFT) Director Sam Raimi peruses some storyboards for an upcoming scene on the infamous Yellow Brick Road. Photograph by Merie Wallace.

(TOP RIGHT) Zach Braff (left), James Franco (middle), and Joey King (right) rehearse a scene in which their characters approach the Dark Forest. Photograph by Merie Wallace.

As secretive as the art department is regarding the exact color of the Yellow Brick Road, the ingredients that came together to design the Land of Oz are anything but mysterious. As Stromberg states: "The most important process on any show is getting the right team together, and we had the right team on this one. Creating this world was a group effort." In the recipe that is the design of *Oz The Great and Powerful*, you'll find a lot of components including: Dechant, Cherniawsky, Jones, McFadyen, Booth, Silvestri, Rogers, Contreras, Wight, Cole, Messing, Bach, Moen, Martinez, two scoops of Manser, Bartoli, Tschetter, Kadonaga, Markwith, Reeder, Smith, Donaldson, Kinter, Wuu, Levine, Frey, Dardas, Lampl, Frost, Mahakian, Engle, Good, Bunikiewicz, Bunker, Radomski, Shank, Costa, Jones, and Oglesby. You'll also find generous portions of Baum, Denslow, Disney, and Raimi. But, the one ingredient that permeates the entire design formula is Stromberg.

Executive producer Palak Patel sums it up succinctly: "No one builds better worlds than Robert Stromberg."

THE YELLOW TILES that comprised the Yellow Brick Road in *Oz The Great and Powerful*. Photograph by John Lord Booth III.

MUNCHKIN STUDY by Michael Kutsche.

CHAPTER III

CREATING
THE COSTUMES
OF OZ

THE GREAT AND POWERFUL

CLOTHING AN ECLECTIC CAST
OF THOUSANDS

"The level of creativity coupled with the sheer magnitude of work costume designers Gary Jones and Michael Kutsche did on this film was astounding. They designed and clothed everyone from an eighteen-inch girl made of china, to an army of eight-foot-tall Winkie guards. And, along the way, they brought to life some of the most iconic and unique characters ever created in American fiction."

GRANT CURTIS, *executive producer*

EXECUTING A CREATIVE VISION

Costumes. As an audience, we sometimes take them for granted. We find ourselves enamored with an actor or wooed by a world. Our hearts swell with the music and our souls dip with the lighting. Yet one of the most important parts of a film, the part that sets it in a time or place, grounds an actor in a role and dictates the tone, is costume design. A well-designed costume makes an actor stand up taller when called for, or fade into the background when needed. The costumes created by the talented Gary Jones and Michael Kutsche for *Oz The Great and Powerful* are, in a word, stunning. Together, the two have created attire that serves to shape a world that is both familiar and new.

Jones and Kutsche are no strangers to working on big-budget tentpole films. Jones' resume includes *The Talented Mr. Ripley*, for which he received an Oscar nomination for Best Costume Design, *The English Patient*, and *Spider-Man 2*, to name a few. Although his past work comprises some of the most revered films ever made, there was one genre that had eluded him. "I realized that I had never experienced the joy of working in a land of sheer fantasy," he states. "Although *Oz The Great and Powerful* is based in some reality, it is a whimsical world. We embraced that and the experience became bigger than life and even more spectacular."

Kutsche also enjoyed working in the fantasy genre, a subset in which he has consistently excelled. The German native, who is a self-taught artist, first came to Hollywood's attention when he was hired as a character designer for Tim Burton's *Alice in Wonderland*. The movie went on to win an Academy Award for Best Costume Design and allowed Kutsche, who had never worked in movies before, an entrance into an elite world. He followed up his work on *Alice* with *John Carter* and *Thor*. *Oz The Great and Powerful*, however, provided him with a slight change to his usual routine. While originally hired to be a character designer, he ultimately ended up conceiving the costumes as well, working with Jones to clothe characters from script to screen.

(TOP) Costume Designer Gary Jones talks with James Franco.

(BOTTOM) Costume Designer Michael Kutsche in the "Room of Resplendence" set.

Kutsche, who views character design like being "an archaeologist," had to do a lot of digging to craft costumes for the four principal characters, as well as a handful of other main characters, and one small flying monkey named Finley. He spent time researching images of monkeys, observing their anatomy and movements in order to accurately portray Finley and ensure that he looked real, yet also fit in the fantasy world of Oz. "You have an image in mind which is the most classic or most cliché," comments Kutsche. "And then you study a real monkey's hand and how odd they are in shape."

Jones likewise did in-depth studies, although he focused more on the real world. "We did extensive research at the Western Costume Company library in Los Angeles, and focused on the years from 1880 through 1930. Those were the years Sam wanted to stay within. We began by looking at circuses and life in the Midwest during that era because that is where and when our film opens, and it is the most grounded part of the story. We researched everything from the largest circus available to traveling circuses in the European tradition. It was a really fascinating journey, and also visually, a huge boon for the picture. One of the unique things we found was that, except for a couple of high-end instances and some period publications, the clothes of those farmers and those people were very utilitarian and only changed slightly during that span of time."

(TOP) A Michael Kutsche illustration of Finley.

(BOTTOM) Kansas wardrobes, inspired by Gary Jones' research. Photograph by Merie Wallace.

shows that began to crisscross Europe around the twelfth century. In many ways the costumes are only different in that they are made with modern materials and different ideas about construction, but the costumes have remained, for all intents and purposes, the same. They evolved from the trick the performer was trying and have been passed down through the ages. The circus environment, and its intricacies, was very personal for me, and I was thrilled to be able to bring that forward."

(THIS PAGE) Circus performer costumes that emerged from in-depth research by the costume department. Photographs by Merie Wallace.

In a fortunate stroke of serendipity for the film, at one point Jones himself worked for the Ringling Bros. and Barnum & Bailey circus. This experience helped inform the earlier scenes of the movie, when the audience sees Oz as a con man, surrounded by the flashiness of carnival life. "I think my past experience had a lot to do with the way I approached this show in that the circus—the artifice of it, the magic, the sleight of hand—is something that Oz himself embodies," comments Jones. "This influence goes back to the traveling

Together, Jones and Kutsche were responsible for a staggering number of costume and character designs. The process started when Kutsche received a call from production designer Robert Stromberg. The pair had worked together on *Alice in Wonderland*, and Stromberg was again in need of Kutsche's creative talents. Kutsche agreed to work on several concepts, focusing first on Finley. "I always start with pencil sketches before I do anything on the computer or with color. You'll go back to the sketch and it tells you the spirit that you had in mind and keeps you on track," explains Kutsche. "I try to design a concept as finished as I can and then present it to the director so that there is a clear vision of the character."

WOODEN HORSE (bottom left), River Fairy (top), and Flying Baboon General (bottom right) illustrations by Michael Kutsche.

Raimi and Stromberg agreed with Kutsche's interpretation of Finley and soon his in-box was full of Baum creations needing attention. "Michael's drawings depicted characters in their costumes playing a moment from the picture, and they were fantastic," comments Raimi. "Right off the bat he had a vision for the picture that fit in with Robert's environment. Like Robert, he's a visionary and his characters really sprang to life out of those drawings."

To bring the designs of Baum, Denslow, Jones, Kutsche, Raimi, and Stromberg to life, Gary and his team (which included assistant costume designers Jessica Peel-Scott and Gali Noy, costume supervisor John Casey, and key costumer Tony Velasco) embarked on an exhaustive process that eventually clothed over 1,500 actors, from 41 inches tall (Munchkin Kristin Riley) to 86 inches tall (Cowboy/Winkie Nik Dragicevic), over a twenty-three-week period. For the principal characters alone, there were well over two hundred pieces.

With Kutsche feverishly sketching in his studio, Jones joined the team and solidified the creative equation. "Sam, Robert, and Michael had started establishing a vocabulary," Jones reflects. "Michael had illustrated the characters and costumes beautifully. I came in and took these wonderful and helpful ideas and fleshed them out literally and figuratively with Sam and Robert".

(TOP LEFT) The wardrobe team created costumes for an array of characters, from Munchkins to towering Winkies, shown here on Tony Cox and Stephen Hart. All photographs on this page by Merie Wallace.

(TOP RIGHT) Emerald City dwellers in their elaborate attire.

(BOTTOM) Quadling children showcase their detailed outfits.

To accomplish such a Herculean feat, the costume department printed, dyed, and beaded fabrics by hand, sorted through warehouses full of old costumes, meticulously painted gold and silver leaf onto white duck feathers, and created and assembled what is arguably one of the most extensive and unique collections of bags, hats, clothes, and whimsical accoutrements ever captured on film. It was, as Jones says with a smile, "a bit outrageous."

Outrageous or not, the effort paid off, resulting in a collection of costumes that will not only pay homage to Baum's original creation, but also bring *Oz The Great and Powerful* into a world all its own.

PHOTOGRAPH by Merie Wallace.

A WIZARD'S WARDROBE

It is somewhat of a rarity to have your main character wear the same costume throughout the entire film, but that was just the case for James Franco on *Oz The Great and Powerful*. As Grant Curtis, the film's executive producer says, "The costume is so subtle and well executed that it becomes imperceptible. That's a real testament to Gary and Michael's design in that you remain in the story—the audience isn't sitting there thinking, 'When's this guy going to change?' That sounds easy to pull off, but it's actually very challenging to achieve."

To bring Oz's seemingly simplistic wardrobe to the big screen, a lot of thought and time was dedicated to the endeavor. "It was a big decision and Sam had a very clear idea of what he wanted," Jones explains. "For Oz to look authentic and of that period — even if he had different pieces of clothing— they would all naturally need to look somewhat similar. So, after a lot of tests and designs, we realized the best thing for the story and Oz's character was to keep a classic design and then give the odd flourish to subtly alter the basic look."

While some actors would balk at having a singular look, as costumes often help define a role, James Franco agreed with Raimi and Jones' vision to stay simple from the start. Gary and James initially met in a coffee shop in New York City where Jones showed Franco several pictures of men from the turn of the century—Alexander Graham Bell, the Wright brothers—to give a sense of the look he had in mind. This preliminary meeting was followed by a series of collaborative encounters in which Franco tried on various suits of different styles and shapes until Oz's ensemble began to take form. However, it wasn't until right before shooting commenced that the vest, jacket, and pants combo that would ultimately form the complete outfit was perfected.

OZ'S SIMPLE BUT ELEGANT cutaway, turn of the century suit, as envisioned by artists Alan Villanueva (this page) and E.J. Krisor (opposite page, left), compared to the final version in the film (opposite page, right). Photograph by Merie Wallace.

"Every time we would go in and add a little something, or explore a little change, usually we rejected it," recalls Jones. "We kept going back to those early conversations and, in the end, it really paid off. I have to admit, it's the costume I'm most proud of. It is a black cutaway suit from the turn of the century and it seamlessly services so many different moods and situations over the course of the film."

TRANSFORMING THEODORA

Perhaps the most challenging character to design for was Theodora. While she starts the film as an innocent and naive young woman with a big heart and high hopes, she ultimately ends up a bitter, broken witch. "Theodora was actually the first costume design I did on the film. There was a little inscription in the script about her wearing pants and having a white dress, but other than that I could work freely on the character's look," Michael Kutsche says. The design he speaks of was Theodora's riding outfit. "Even if Oz is a fantasy world, it's still a period piece to a degree. So I was looking at the fashion around 1900 and they had pretty crazy hats. However, I incorporated a more modern kind of jacket. They didn't have this style of jacket in the early 1900s. Theodora's is more contemporary, so it's a patchwork of different periods that make it look like it lacks a distinct period. That's what creates its slightly fantastical feel."

"Theodora has quite a journey," declares Jones. "In the beginning it was really important that she be accessible and sexy. And I think that we accomplished that by taking some liberties with the period, the fabrics, and the way we put it all together. This approach flowed beautifully through to her dinner dress in a very nice way. I love that dress."

Riding habits and dinner dresses aside, Theodora's most important costume is, not surprisingly, her witch's outfit. "I started off by embracing her youth, because it's almost thirty years before the original story," Kutsche says. "So she was not hunched over and really contained. Sam asked me to put a little sexiness and sort of spirit and energy into her. It was quite a journey."

EARLY EXPLORATIONS of Theodora's riding outfit (this page), ball gown (opposite page, left), and her look as Wicked Witch of the West (opposite page, right). Illustrations by Michael Kutsche.

OZ

THEODORA EVENING DRESS v01
MARCH 9 2011

OZ

WICKED THEODORA v16
APRIL 18 2011

The result of Kutsche and Jones' journey produced a witch that is more modern and structured than ever. To achieve this modernity while at the same time accentuating the Witch's wickedness, intricately tooled black leather was embraced from head to toe, as well as some key accessories. Talons were infused into the shoulder design to give the Witch a more menacing feel, and a unique balaclava-like scarf was embraced. "I put the black scarf around her and it really made it seem as if her face was floating in darkness," states Kutsche. "There's something iconic to it, and I kind of got there by accident, but it really works."

THE FINAL LOOK of the Wicked
Witch of the West as seen in the film.

ESTABLISHING EVANORA'S ENSEMBLE

"Evanora wound up having fewer costumes than we had planned," Jones says of his work on the Wicked Witch hailing from the East, "but I feel strongly that we brought a really iconic look to her design. Her beauty, as a character, is a little on the flashy side, and she's also quite deceitful. The designs of her dresses play right into that."

To get across that combination of beauty and wickedness, Jones and Kutsche relied on a combination of colors and construction. "The starting point for me with Evanora's outfit was the Art Deco architecture of Emerald City," Kutsche notes. "Her costume worked in conjunction with—not separate from—the world found in Rob's drawings and the drawings from the art department. There was a certain logic to his designs that I wanted to reflect in my illustrations—and by resembling and reflecting that, I could make her more of a mighty being that stands out against all the other citizens, and the other witches as well. That is why you'll find a lot of similar lines and shapes if you compare the two." Adds Jones, "In the Emerald City, the people are a little more oppressed, and that informed Evanora's dress, which has stronger, more ominous colors—some blacks, some grays."

With the Emerald City itself as a starting point, Kutsche created an original character design with an iconic silhouette that signified Evanora's power and strength. When she first appears, her dress is a deep green that mirrors the city around her and emphasizes her role as current ruler of the Emerald City.

Jones responded strongly to this design, but there was some further experimentation in regard to color, style, and structure. At one point the overall approach veered toward a look more reminiscent of the Duchess of Windsor, and another study fleshed out the idea of having her in white at the beginning, but that was seen as too pure. A pale green followed, which was then darkened to mirror her darker nature. Ultimately, the exploration went full circle and the team came back to Kutsche's original concept, creating the mercury green dress, as well as a gray-black dress that she appears in for the second half of the film.

MICHAEL KUTSCHE'S designs for Evanora (opposite page and top) had to include both her look as the beautiful royal advisor and as a decrepit hag.

(BOTTOM RIGHT) Rachel Weisz as Evanora.

THE GOWNS OF GLINDA
THE GOOD WITCH OF THE SOUTH

For *Oz The Great and Powerful*, Gary Jones and Michael Kutsche were assigned the task of re-imagining Glinda's iconic costume while staying true to what originally made the character so special in Baum's adventures.

MICHAEL KUTSCHE'S design for Glinda in both early sketch and final illustration form.

ONE OF THE GOOD WITCH'S

dresses as it appears in its final form.

Luckily, inspiration came from the world that production designer Robert Stromberg had been crafting. In creating Glinda's castle and kingdom, Stromberg had implemented a pearlescent sheen that could be found in everything from the bubbles she floated in to the wallpaper in her library. Jones and Kutsche brought that pearlescence into her costumes, layering different shades of white to create the depth found in her surroundings. "Glinda's first dress and her warrior dress are translucent and opaque," Jones explains. "They incorporate shades of white, opalescent white,

cream, and silver, and they have some birdlike qualities. Michelle [Williams], Sam, and I liked the idea of her being able to fly away. The opalescent colors of the bubble were wonderful to explore, and I think that in the end they really paid off with her final dress."

Ultimately, the costumes created for Glinda the Good Witch of the South stand out as fresh and original. They breathe new life into a character that has been the epitome of the perfect princess for generations.

OUTFITTING ODDBALLS

The world of Oz is populated by a variety of inhabitants. There are Munchkins, who can be found in both the Emerald City and Glinda's kingdom, and Quadlings, who live peacefully and happily under Glinda's rule out in the country. Then there are Tinkers, an assortment of old men who are capable of building anything, and eight-foot-tall Winkies who guard the Emerald City and protect its citizens from impending villainy. Each group is as unique as their name, which means each one needed a look equally distinctive.

(BOTTOM LEFT) Three members of the design team (left to right) Tony Velasco, Gary Jones, and John Casey, who helped make the costumes a reality. Photograph by Merie Wallace.

(TOP RIGHT) Munchkin designs by Michael Kutsche.

"The game plan was to try and separate the country folk from the city folk with color," Jones says of how he and Kutsche tackled the costume design for these groups. "The in-town Quadlings wore grays and blues and cool colors with accents of many other colors. Everyone had a little flower or a dash of green, but then the country Quadlings were in earth tones—browns, gold, harvest colors—and they were slightly less extreme in every way. With the residents of Emerald City, we exaggerated all of the different accessories and trimming, almost in a graphic way. You really see the buttons or the outline of a collar because of a certain trim that's on it. Those things all became very important."

Color was not the only thing the designers thought of when working to create the people of Oz. Shape was also very important. "The shapes were really exaggerated, turn of the century shapes," Jones says. Kutsche initially drew sketches where accessories were exaggerated and fancified, but Sam wanted to push it even further. "So a shoe that appeared to have a pointed toe became very pointed," Jones explains. "The skirts were not just puffy, they were melonlike. Everything got pushed further than even our witches, or our leading man, or any of their costumes. These characters became more extreme."

Working on Munchkins and Winkies was itself an experiment in extremes: the Munchkins are small while the Winkies are decidedly large. "We started making clothes that were real and within the framework of the drawing prototypes that Michael had done. Then we started fitting people and taking their various sizes and shapes into account, and we accommodated all of that within the real clothing designs. I think that plays out very well in the way they look."

KNUCK V2
OZ: THE GREAT AND POWERFUL
5.13.2011
ALAN VILLANUEVA

THE MUNCHKINS rehearse a stunt in the film (bottom left, photograph by Merie Wallace) and a character sketch of Knuck by Alan Villanueva (top).

SEVERAL LOOKS for the
Quadlings—all vastly different
and yet contributing to the
cohesive look of the background
characters. Photographs by Chris
Williams and Merie Wallace.

SAMPLING of the intricately adorned citizenry of the Emerald City. Photographs by Chris Williams and Merie Wallace.

TINKER ILLUSTRATIONS by
Michael Kutsche (left) and Victor
Martinez (right).

THE MUNCHKINS on set.
Photographs by Merie Wallace.

On the other end of the height spectrum were the Winkies. While Jones and Kutsche faced a different challenge in trying to create outfits that did not look too cartoonish and were grounded in reality for the Munchkins, creating the Winkies proved slightly easier. "They were really fun," Jones says of his work on the Winkies. "Their costumes were some of the first things we had approved and were inspired by Russian and Prussian military uniforms. We had any number of prototypes working and testing, but we came back to the shape that Michael had originally illustrated." As the Guards of the Emerald City, the Winkies have a bit less individuality to their costumes. They are uniform and provide an important part of the story. This uniformity of character made for a striking image on-screen. "Once they were all together and marching, it was one of those great shivers up your spine moments," Jones says.

As spine-tingling and unique as all the designs Jones and Kutsche created were, there was one aspect they contained that proved more important than any other – synergy with the environment around them and the characters they clothed. As strange as it may seem, the true success of their vision is that their designs don't stand out in context. Kutsche's described approach for Evanora—working in conjunction with, not apart from, the design of the entire film—was one that informed their approach to each of the approximately 1,500 characters they clothed. Granted Jones and Kutsche's designs solo at the appropriate moments, but for the most part, the true genius of the film's costumes is that they masterfully blend with the fanciful orchestra around them.

(TOP RIGHT) Winkie Guard illustration by Michael Kutsche.

(BOTTOM LEFT) The Winkie uniforms lined up on costume racks. Photograph by Merie Wallace.

(BOTTOM RIGHT) Stephen Hart as the Winkie General. Photograph by Chris Williams.

16 FEET
15 FEET
14 FEET
13 FEET
12 FEET
11 FEET
10 FEET
9 FEET
8 FEET
7 FEET
6 FEET
5 FEET
4 FEET
3 FEET
2 FEET
1 FOOT

SPECIAL MAKEUP EFFECTS SUPERVISOR
Howard Berger touches up Mila Kunis'
Wicked Witch look before a take.
Photograph by Merie Wallace.

CHAPTER IV

THE MAGICAL ADVENTURE THROUGH
THE ART OF MAKEUP

WRITTEN BY HOWARD BERGER,
SPECIAL MAKEUP EFFECTS SUPERVISOR

"Howard is great—he doesn't impose a design that doesn't exist. He takes his raw materials and lets them bloom and develop beautifully. And, all the actors love working with him. It's difficult living under that makeup for hours and hours, but Howard's always on top of it, seeing to the details, making sure it's kept up and looks perfect for every shot."

SAM RAIMI, *director*

December 12, 2011
Day 100
3:00a.m.

I enter Michigan Motion Picture Studios in Pontiac, Michigan, as I have been doing for the past six months. The mornings are early and the days are long. My entire team of top gun makeup artists is always right behind me. No matter what time it is or what is asked of them, they perform their magic every day like a well-oiled tin man.

We hit the power on our makeup stations and the lights illuminate the tools of our trade—makeup brushes, tattoo color pallets, sponges, scissors, adhesives, powder puffs, you name it. On the tables behind each makeup station are stacked hundreds of silicone and foam rubber prosthetics for our cast of Ozian characters. There are white plastic vacuform faces that support each prosthetic piece. Munchkin noses of different shapes, some small, some ski jumped, some bulbous. Boxes of pointed Tinker ears, all painted and the rims of the ears lined with a soft fuzz to add realism. Stacks of pre-painted Winkie chins, noses, foreheads, and cheeks are ready to be applied to the eight-foot-tall actors playing the Witch's guards. Thousands of finely manicured mustaches, beards, and sideburns line the walls of the makeup rooms, each pinned to a photo of the corresponding actor they belong to.

The task each day is overwhelming and arduous, but unbelievably rewarding and exciting. We all wait with anticipation for the first actors to sit in our chairs when we are able to begin the magical transformation from a human actor into their character in the wonderful Land of Oz!

But, before any of this ever gets to this stage, everything has to be designed, sculpted, fabricated, manufactured, and brought to life. This is where my studio, KNB EFX GROUP, comes into play! My business partner, Greg Nicotero, and I first worked with Sam Raimi back in 1986 on *Evil Dead II*. We fell in love with him at first sight and knew we had to work with him on every film he ever directed. His energy, enthusiasm, teamwork, and respect for what each person brought to the table are overwhelming and something very rare in this business. When we caught word that Sam was gearing up to do a prequel to *The Wonderful Wizard of Oz*, well, we had to be involved.

SPECIAL MAKEUP EFFECTS SUPERVISOR
Howard Berger.

Wicked Theodora
Mila Kunis
Stage 3k

WHEATON
2011

(THIS PAGE) The makeup design for the Wicked Witch. Illustration by John Wheaton.

(OPPOSITE PAGE) Knuck (Tony Cox) gets a touch-up by Peter Montagna before a take. Photograph by Merie Wallace.

We began designing in December 2010. Our key designer, John Wheaton, worked alongside the great Bernie Wrightson and Jordu Schell to help visualize the cast of characters we needed to create for the film. John worked his magic in Photoshop focusing on Munchkins and witches; Bernie provided some beautiful and expressive line illustrations of witches; and Jordu came up with the most amazing flying monkey study sculpture I had ever seen. It was all fantastic and inspiring. We presented the artwork to Sam and he loved it, feeling we were heading down the right path. I think at the end of the day we probably produced over two hundred pieces of art for these characters.

The next step was to get actors in for life casts so we could begin sculpting the custom prosthetics. The first actor cast was the lovely and talented Mila Kunis. Here was a woman with one of the most gorgeous faces in the world. Those eyes, those lips, and I had to turn her into the Wicked Theodora. I knew I wanted to keep as much of Mila as possible. John Wheaton did some great design work for her character based on photos I had taken of her. They ranged from very subtle to extreme. I wanted to go as extreme as we could, but I had this feeling that the studio would say, "We want to see her face!"

I took all of the designs to the set, and showed Sam and Mila at the same time. Sam, who is always very cautious about every decision, took some time reviewing each piece. He would pick up each design and study it. Nodding, he would put it down and move onto the next. I waited with anticipation to see which one he liked when I heard Mila say, "I like this one!" She was pointing to the most extreme and at that point I knew Ms. Kunis and I would be friends forever. A girl after my own heart. She went right to the monster! Sam held the piece Mila was pointing to and after about five minutes of silence said, "Hey buddy, yeah, this is the one!" I had my witch!

At KNB we have the greatest artists in the film industry. Jeremy Aiello, Norman Cabrera, Alex Diaz, Garrett Immel, Andy Schoenberg, Kevin Wasner, and Nick Marra made up our crack team of sculptors. Norman and Andy sculpted Mila's makeup. Nick handled Rachel Weisz's "hag" version of Evanora, to which Sam said: "It's my best hag yet!" Garrett sculpted the many different looks on actor Stephen Hart, who would be the point of reference for the look of the Winkies.

Mark Boley and his team of hair designers and stylists handled the five hundred-plus handmade wigs and facial hairpieces. They worked nonstop hand-tying dozens of Tinker beards and wigs.

Jim Leonard, our mold supervisor, and his team produced hundreds of urethane resin molds for the prosthetic manufacturing division, led by Derek Krout, as he and Steve Katz produced thousands of silicone and foam rubber prosthetics. The count was actually over three thousand pieces run during the prep and while filming began, as the final tally of applied makeups on the show came in at 2,700 makeups. That's a lot of silicone and foam rubber!

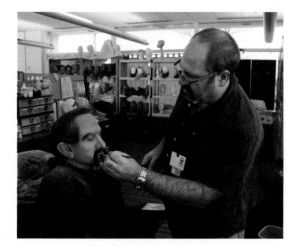

After a five-month preproduction period, we were ready to head off to location and start the next portion of our Oz journey. Peter Montagna, who is one of the best people in the industry, was my right hand the entire show. I could not have asked for a better person, artist, and friend to stand beside me and help mastermind the entire operation. Peter has this very calm and collected sense about him. He is amazingly confident and never gets frazzled. I pride myself on these qualities too, but Pete puts me to shame.

My key team of makeup artists consisted of Gino Crognale, Garrett Immel, Michael Mills, Greg Nelson, Robert Kurtzman, and Kenny Diaz. They were in the main makeup room where Peter and I were. This was the room we shared with the head of the makeup department, Vivian Baker. Vivian is the sweetest Georgia peach of a person. Her Southern demeanor makes you want to give her a big hug every time you hear her voice welcome you into the room. "Morning, darlin'," she says with a slight Southern drawl. Vivian and her amazing team of artists—Steven Anderson, Georgia Allen, Bree Shea, and Steve LaPorte—are all top-notch. They can do anything from specifically designed beauty makeups for the Quadlings, to hand-tying three hundred Emerald City residence mustaches with a multitude of colors subtly woven into the design. Vivian had a hand in every single makeup her department produced for the film. I would come in at three in the morning to start Mila's makeup, and there was Vivian sitting cross-legged on the floor, a hot cup of tea in her hands, as she reviewed every single facial hairpiece to make sure it was the way she wanted it. She is very specific about everything and pays great attention to the smallest of things, which is a tribute to her dedication and perfectionism to the art of makeup.

(THIS PAGE) Prosthetics are applied to Munchkin Rebel Martin Klebba (left) and a Winkie (right).

(OPPOSITE PAGE) A continuity assemblage of Kansas turn of the century mustaches. Photograph by Merie Wallace.

Peter Montagna was Tony Cox's makeup artist. Tony plays Evanora's Munchkin servant Knuck. We knew we wanted to keep as much as we could of Tony's own face, as the trick with any prosthetic makeup is, less is more. We did not want to have too much on him, as we wanted his facial expressions to read through as part of his performance. In the end, Peter applied small silicone cheek pieces to give him a more rounded, apple-cheeked look, a nose tip, ears, and a small brow piece; that was a common thread in the designs of the Munchkins that I wanted to carry through, to have this very specific brow shape that would make them feel more sympathetic and inquisitive. Out in the bull pen—that is what we call the area where you have the rest of your makeup and hairstylists working together—it's very Old Hollywood. As a kid, I would look at books that had photos of studio stages converted into big makeup corrals, known as bull pens, and I would think, "How cool. I hope I get to be a part of that someday!" In our bull pen, Vivian had about twenty makeup artists doing their magic. Yolanda Toussieng, our brilliant hair designer, had around fifteen stylists, and our department had thirty artists. Early on, Peter and I

sat down and made a wish list of the best of the best and figured, "Why not? Let's shoot for the moon." Well, we got them all. Artists from all eras, all my idols from when I was a kid reading the monster and makeup magazines. We had Leonard Engelman, Craig Reardon, Kevin Haney, Mark Landon, Stephan Dupuis, and Margret Prentice to name a few. I also got to bring on fellow artists from my generation, some of whom I have known for decades—Greg Funk, Ozzy Alvarez, Lee Grimes, Jamie Kelman, David Dupuis, Joe Podnar—and some I had always wanted to work with, like Richie Alonzo, Toni G., Jonah Levy, Danny Wagner, Connor McCullagh, and Richard Redlefsen.

We had a great team, and that is what it was—a team—
that worked together to make the adventure into Oz a
magical one. I always feel it is so important to enjoy
what you do and have a great time while you are doing
it. I look for projects that challenge us at KNB and
the team I am working with, and in *Oz The Great and
Powerful* I could not have asked for a greater journey and
adventure, as it was a once-in-a-lifetime opportunity.

(THIS PAGE) Martin Klebba
poses as a Rebel Munchkin.

(OPPOSITE PAGE) The bull
pen where the makeup and hair
teams worked together to prep
the hundreds of actors who
appeared in the movie.

(THESE PAGES) A gallery of
the special makeup effects
team's work on the film.

MAKEUP DEPARTMENT HEAD
Vivian Baker (this page, top left,
and opposite page, bottom left)
and her team apply the intricate
makeup on Quadling actors.
Photographs by Merie Wallace.

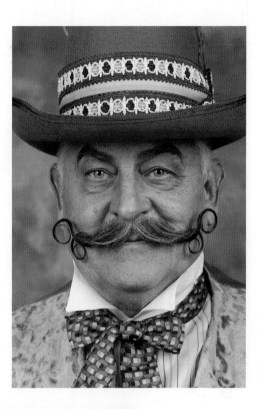

A **SAMPLE.** of the many faces and hairstyles in *Oz The Great and Powerful.*

THE WICKED WITCHES look toward a computer-generated Emerald City and fireworks show in this final frame from the movie.

CHAPTER V

DELIVERING THE LAND OF OZ THE GREAT AND POWERFUL

A VISUAL EFFECTS TALE OF TWO WIZARDS

"I think the visual effects industry is reaching a level of maturity where it isn't about the latest lighting techniques or cameras. It's more about the artistry and the craft. On Oz The Great and Powerful, we're using the latest techniques, but we've made a lot of key decisions in how we execute the shots in order to make this a timeless visual effects movie, as opposed to the latest, greatest, technological extravaganza."

SCOTT STOKDYK, *visual effects supervisor*

On *Oz The Great and Powerful*, a creative perfect storm presented itself that relied heavily on the talents of one department to bind multiple elements together. Baum's vision, Denslow's whimsy, Stromberg's genius, Kapner and Lindsay-Abaire's ingenuity, and Raimi's all-encompassing wizardry combined to form a visual vortex whose execution ultimately landed on the doorstep of the visual effects department.

The filmmakers' collective imagination fashioned a fantastical land that would make Mother Nature green with envy. Furthermore, it was partially populated by a cast of characters only the digital age could bring to fruition. To deliver such a land to the silver screen, replete with the added technical challenges and creative opportunities that accompany a 3-D presentation, the talents of a world-class visual effects team would need to be called upon. A team with an expertise in photo-real world creation; the proven ability to create, animate, and integrate realistic characters into a live-action environment; and a pressure-tested unflappability when designing, constructing, and delivering some of the most complicated visual effects ever created.

With such intricate prerequisites, the list of potential VFX suitors was short, but distinguished. However, one entrant rose above the rest. Having previously made some of the most respected and groundbreaking visual effects films in motion picture history, Sony Pictures Imageworks emerged as the clear choice to realize Sam Raimi and Robert Stromberg's vision of L. Frank Baum's creation.

Leading the charge for SPI is Academy Award-winning VFX supervisor Scott Stokdyk and Troy Saliba, one of the most sought-after animation supervisors in the industry. Their reflections on the process of delivering the visual effects elements for *Oz The Great and Powerful* offer a unique insight into one of the most dichotomous departments in filmmaking. Their responsibilities run the gamut, from the extraordinarily creative to the extremely technical, and in-between you will find one of the most vital components in modern cinema.

VFX SUPERVISOR Scott Stokdyk captures set reference to inform a digital shot (top). Photograph by Merie Wallace. Animation supervisor Troy Saliba models a pair of wings he crafted for an on-set scale representation of Finley's CG wings (bottom). Photograph by Scott Stokdyk.

FINLEY THE FLYING MONKEY in his fully realized, CG form.

A CONVERSATION WITH
SCOTT STOKDYK
AND TROY SALIBA

GRANT CURTIS: *Scott, generally speaking, what does a visual effects supervisor do?*

SCOTT STOKDYK: I'm responsible for overseeing the execution of the visual effects in the movie—visual effects being images created through means other than traditional live-action photography. In recent years, our craft has been dominated by computer-generated imagery, but it still encompasses numerous complex disciplines, such as models and miniatures, motion control, compositing, time-lapse, blue screen and multiple pass photography, and matte painting.

For me, the visual effects process usually begins in preproduction, where there is only a script for guidance, and continues through the final delivery of the film to theaters. Along the way I use discussions with the director and collaborate with other movie department heads to figure out the best way to bring this digital imagery to the screen. On a large movie like *Oz The Great and Powerful*, it would be impossible for me to do this without a very capable visual effects producer to organize and manage the process, while tracking the budget and schedules for the multiple companies who work on the movie. Tamara Watts Kent is the visual effects producer on *Oz The Great and Powerful*, and she has been fantastic.

MEMBERS of the camera and sound teams race to keep up with James Franco and Zach Braff as the company films a chase scene.

GRANT CURTIS: *Troy, as the animation supervisor you oversee and bring a cohesive look to all the animated elements in the film. What skill sets do you look for in an animator when building your team?*

TROY SALIBA: The best animators are the ones that can cross over. They can animate something that is very punchy and stylized, but they can also seamlessly transition to photo-real shots. And, within photo-real sequences, they can deliver performance-based talking characters, and the aspects of a shot that necessitate dynamic physics—elements that require a lot of power and weight to them.

An animator's objectivity is also crucial. You have to learn to view your work as if it's not your own—don't get precious about it. Be able to stand back and study it with somebody else's eyes and see if it's hitting the main points you need to deliver. If you can develop that skill where you can coldly and clinically

look at your own work, you'll be ahead of the game. But, that's a very hard thing for people to do. Even seasoned animators sometimes find it difficult to take that extra leap in order to view their work in the context of the big picture—how does a particular shot fit into the film as a whole? What are the needs of the director, the needs of the production? Objectivity is something I really value in a senior animator.

JAMES FRANCO on set in Pontiac, Michigan (this page), and overlooking an Oz landscape (opposite page), with the aid of the talented team at Sony Pictures Imageworks.

GRANT CURTIS: *They also have to be able to emote with their pen.*

TROY SALIBA: Of course, but it's not just an acting sense that they need to have. They also have to understand 2-D composition and how to graphically stage their character in frame so that the audience is looking where they are supposed to look. And all this while maintaining a consistent aesthetic—every film has its own aesthetic sensibility.

Then, there's the camera. A good animator needs to know what the camera is doing and how that affects their character. On this show we deal with both full CG shots, where we have complete control and the flexibility to go in and place cameras and characters where need be. But we also work with existing photography, where the camera moves and other characters in the frame are already baked in. That's where a lot of creativity comes in—when the artist has to work with existing components he or she had no control over and make his or her character or elements work.

GRANT CURTIS: *You are both quite accomplished and have a variety of opportunities to choose from. What attracted you to this project?*

SCOTT STOKDYK: Being a visual effects supervisor, I'm always attracted to opportunities to create unique and interesting visuals. *Oz The Great and Powerful* had those, as well as a fascinating combination of significant VFX challenges and a distinct style.

Also, since I'm typically committing myself to two or more years for a VFX-intensive film, it's very important to me to be working with people I like and respect. Collaborating with Sam is always a wonderful opportunity on all levels—he is one of the few directors who has both a great visual style and an interest in telling an emotionally engaging story. Sam is also a genuinely great person to work with on a personal level—after *Oz The Great and Powerful,* I will have worked with him for over nine years.

TROY SALIBA: For me, it was three things. I worked with Scott before on *G-Force* and had a really great experience. He's one of my favorite VFX supervisors. Not only is he incredibly experienced, skilled, and talented, but he's also collaborative in a way that invites you into every part of the process that has anything to do with characters. On many films it's a little more segregated. Sometimes, the character design and its 3-D execution is handled by someone else. But Scott inserts you into the process right away and fosters an environment where you can develop a good relationship with the director and the producers. That is really refreshing.

MILA KUNIS as the Wicked Witch stands atop a partial set (opposite page) and atop the Emerald City in a final frame from the film (this page).

Another factor was that Sam was directing the project. I did a little bit of animation on *Spider-Man 2* and had a lot of fun with that. So, I was looking forward to working with him again, especially at this level where I worked closely with him on set and helped design the work flow that delivered his movie to the big screen.

The final factor was simply the product itself. You get to help make the world of Oz fresh, and at the same time allow people to feel like they are home again.

GRANT CURTIS: *Speaking of the Oz title, were either of you familiar with L. Frank Baum's Oz books before you started this film?*

SCOTT STOKDYK: Having grown up in Kansas, I endured a lot of good-natured ribbing about Oz when I moved to California. It was an obligation to be familiar with all things Oz when you have that kind of connection. As soon as I started on the movie, I promptly ordered all the books to refamiliarize myself with the world.

GRANT CURTIS: *And what type of research did you do in order to make the world Baum originally envisioned a reality?*

SCOTT STOKDYK: Working in VFX involves a constant state of research. On *Oz The Great and Powerful*, I looked at things like Tesla coil lighting, various magic performances, circus acts, strange natural creatures, and bird-wing evolution.

The research that stands out to me the most, though, was my tornado research. Early in the process, I contacted professional storm-chaser Roger Hill. He offered up an amazing amount of information and reference about not just tornadoes, but the context within which they appear. We even sent VFX photographer Chris Hebert out with Roger on a storm-chasing tour in an effort to get a believable sky that could generate a tornado. The photos Chris took ended up being the source for our sky creation, while images from Roger's photo library were key pieces of inspiration for our CG tornadoes.

A **PHOTOGRAPH** taken by Chris Hebert while storm chasing to capture reference for *Oz The Great and Powerful*.

GRANT CURTIS: *Troy, what was your research and development process like?*

TROY SALIBA: We knew that Finley was a flying monkey and that the Wicked Witch had her evil baboons, so one of the first things we did was hire an animal trainer. He came in one day with a monkey and a couple of baboons—that was a real eye-opener. There is primate reference on the computer, but there's just something about being in the room with these creatures—seeing how they react to things like you trying to make eye contact with them, especially the baboons. They have such a presence. It's like walking into a bar where everyone is agitated. They naturally have this, "You wanna go?" sort of feeling about them. I didn't get that from the reference I had previously seen, and that interaction has fueled a lot of the direction I've given the animators throughout the show.

I also did a lot of Zach Braff research because I knew we were going to take the way monkeys move and communicate, and infuse that with Zach's performance. I watched a lot of his past work so that I could get used to who he is and what he brings to a character.

(THESE PAGES) Early studies by Troy Saliba as he brainstorms Finley facial expressions, and a walking cycle. An early sketch of a winged baboon is also present in his explorations, as well as sketches of Zach Braff, the voice and inspiration behind Finley.

(THESE PAGES) Zach Braff's performance is captured and later incorporated by the VFX crew to make Finley's final facial reactions in the film.

GRANT CURTIS: *And what about China Girl?*

TROY SALIBA: It was challenging because I knew it was something we were going to have to invent. There's no reference out there on how a living, breathing, eighteen-inch girl made of china moves. I did some research and conducted experiments, which helped me decide upon a path I was going to go down, and then Phillip [marionette artist Phillip Huber] came aboard and that changed everything. He's been so instrumental in setting the tone and manner in which the doll moves. There is a lot about the way China Girl performs that is Joey King, but there is a lot that Phillip has contributed as well. Everybody fell in love with what he was doing on set, especially Sam and editor Bob Murawski. Phillip's participation was invaluable because it gave us a really good foundation for how that doll would move.

SCOTT STOKDYK: At first, I hesitated at the idea of having a marionette version of China Girl on set as reference—I thought it would give a good lighting orientation and be an interaction aid for the actors at best. But, after seeing Phillip perform and breathe life into an object with such limits on its motion, the marionette became inspirational.

(THESE PAGES) Marionette artist Phillip Huber puppeteers the China Girl marionette during scenes from the film. Huber's puppet would later be removed digitally, and replaced with the computer-generated version based on Joey King's performance. Photographs by Merie Wallace.

While Finley's animation has a world of possibilities (Zach's performance, monkey behavior, bird behavior), the China Girl is a study in restrictions and discipline in animation. Studying Phillip Huber's performance we learned that the viewer will read emotion into a performance that is held back and subtle. For example, Phillip's marionette has no facial expressions other than some crude eye movement, yet with his forty-plus years of experience he was able to almost make you think the puppet is talking. It's uncanny the way Phillip has overcome the limits of his medium and transcended them, and that became my rallying cry to Troy—can we restrict the China Girl's eyebrow movement and still see her expressions? Can we reduce the range of motion and degrees of freedom of the joints and still achieve the action? Can small movements in the head substitute for eye motions? In fact, some of that philosophy spilled into my thinking about the monkey—could we still read Finley's expressions if the whites of his eyes were darker and more monkey-like? I felt having self-imposed animation restrictions that we would have to overcome would only help us develop something unique for the animation in *Oz The Great and Powerful*.

THE CHINA GIRL
marionette (opposite page)
was used on set for the cast
to act with, and to provide
inspiration to the animators at
Sony Pictures Imageworks who
would later create the final
digital character (this page).

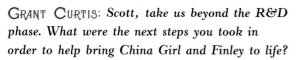

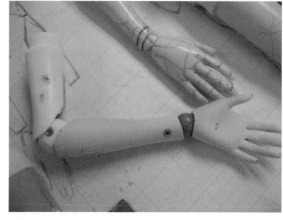

GRANT CURTIS: *Scott, take us beyond the R&D phase. What were the next steps you took in order to help bring China Girl and Finley to life?*

SCOTT STOKDYK: China Girl started from an illustration by costume designer/character designer Michael Kutsche. After talking to Sam, Michael came up with a simple, yet beautiful, concept that feels timeless. His design could work in 1900 as easily as it does in 2013.

Based on that design, Phillip and Howard Berger went about creating a real doll. The KNB team sculpted a design and then made molds out of it. Phillip has a lot of experience making his own marionettes, so he took these molds and made his own version of the China Girl that he could puppet on set as discussed.

At the same time, Troy and the team at Sony Pictures Imageworks made a CG version of the China Girl. It was based on the illustration, the practical puppet, Joey King, and ideas from Troy's

years of experience in animation. After this base-surface model was made in CG, the CG cloth was created to match the marionette's dress made by costume designer Gary Jones, and we had our digital China Girl.

As for Finley, his origins lie in a Michael Kutsche design as well. However, I knew he was going to have to be photo-real, so from the start I went out and found photographs of capuchin monkeys. I was fascinated by the almost humanlike expressiveness and was convinced that we needed a capuchin element in the final Finley design. Specifically, I loved the wrinkles that showed up in the monkey's forehead.

To clarify, China Girl had to be photo-real too, but the human brain knows what a monkey is supposed to look like, which makes it more complicated when creating in CG. It's always easier to generate a digital character that you don't

(THESE PAGES) Phillip Huber delicately creates the China Girl marionette. Photographs by David Alexander.

have a connection to in the natural world such as a robot, or an alien, or a doll made of china. It's much harder to deliver a human or a monkey because the eye automatically knows how that object is supposed to look and move.

To create our CG Finley, we used Michael's illustration as our blueprint. Then, to bring more realism to the character, we acquired textures and design improvements from a photo shoot with a capuchin monkey named Crystal, famous for her role in *The Hangover Part II*. The final piece of the puzzle was Finley's wings. They were based on real birds with elliptical wing-types, which are ideal for tight maneuvering in small spaces. We wanted Finley to be a light, quick creature, as opposed to more predatory birds that tend to glide like eagles or hawks. Photos from specimens at the Natural History Museum [in Los Angeles], in particular the wood pigeon, formed the basis, and we art-directed from there.

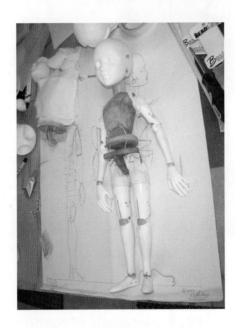

We have a lot of artistic challenges on this movie, the core of which is that we have two virtual characters, China Girl and Finley, who are in many ways the heart of the story. We have fought really hard to make them engaging, emoting, lovable characters that the audience cares about and that have a connection with other actors. Creating and enacting the plan that has brought them to life has been one of the biggest challenges on this film, but also one of the most rewarding.

(THESE PAGES) Joey King's wide range of facial expressions were recorded and used by the VFX crew to make China Girl's final facial reactions in the film.

GRANT CURTIS: *Troy, you discussed your R&D. Once that is complete, can you describe the steps you go through to animate a character?*

TROY SALIBA: Initially, I'll often go in and do a lot of drawings—not so much worrying about the model to come, but just trying to capture the essence of the character and the kind of poses that can be achieved. I'll show those to the director and see what feels good to him or her. This informs some of the extremes we're going to have to accomplish when we start building the model.

In the case of *Oz The Great and Powerful*, the next step was to take Michael's designs and realize them in three dimensions so that we could animate them digitally. You have to set it up so that all the joints are going to work the way you need, with all the physical limitations that you don't have to deal with when you're doing an illustration. There's a lot of inevitable interpretation that goes from a 2-D drawing to a 3-D model. In the computer everything has to work in a practical way. Therefore, elements of the illustration have to be tweaked so that the design can work. You naturally see the drawing and think, "Yep, we just have to go build that." But, then you go in and start to realize: that element of the design doesn't really work in 3-D space; that design aspect in that particular pose is very clear, but as soon as you start rotating the camera around it begins to look like a different character. It's always a steeper learning curve than most people are prepared for.

Once you have the model and everyone feels like it's something you can move forward with, then you start posing it—that's when the character comes to life. And, as you are posing the model, you are starting to interact with it, but in order to take the model to the next level and animate with it, further refinement, called rigging, is necessary.

Rigging is the process in which a technical artist places a "skeleton" inside the model. In doing so, they literally decide where all the joints are going to be, and how all the muscles react when you move the joints. This process takes a really long time, especially when you get into characters with subtle facial performances—which we obviously have.

ANIMATION SUPERVISOR Troy Saliba captures the essence of a flying Finley in this early collection sketched during preproduction.

As soon as the model is rigged, you start experimenting with it. Unsurprisingly, this instigates a lot of discussions like, "When we achieve this specific expression, this part of the model doesn't hold up and therefore the character as a whole is no longer working." You try and test it from every sort of scenario imaginable, both physically and performance-wise, so that by the time you're in production and getting shots in, you know you can handle everything you need to pull off.

While the model is going through these steps, Scott's team is taking the character through a process called look development. This is where they ask and graphically answer all sorts of questions such as: if the character has hair, what does it look like, and how does it move? If they have clothes, what does the texture of the cloth look like, and how does the look of these textures change as the character moves? What does the skin texture look like? Does the character have stubble, or hairs in their ears, or eyelashes? What color are the eyes and how reflective are they going to be? This is an exhaustive process, but as you can imagine, it is the minutia that breathes life into a character.

GRANT CURTIS: *You talk about what seems like an extreme—building a skeleton and interactive musculature within the model so that it has the proper 3-D constraints. Is that necessary? Does the audience perceive it if you cheat those constraints?*

TROY SALIBA: Most definitely. The human eye sees and registers physical constraints almost constantly, and can therefore perceive when those realities are broken. The level of play you have with that depends on a few parameters. One being what Scott discussed earlier—how photo-real is your character and is it based in reality? If you've never seen it before, you have a little more latitude, but even then we have to be very careful about how the joints are placed and how the musculature works so that it all feels acceptable. Another aspect we have to deal with in this movie is the fact that it is 3-D. Cheats that might look good when you're studying them from one lens [2-D], become even more evident in 3-D.

GRANT CURTIS: *When the digital age was ushered in and the predominate animation tool became the computer, a perception emerged that devalued the actual animators. How important is the individual artist in today's CG animation?*

THE PRACTICAL SET of the Room of Resplendence (opposite page) is a feat in and of itself—with property master Russell Bobbitt creating over 5,000 coins for the scene—but the overwhelming decadence of the room truly comes to life with the magic touch of the VFX department (this page).

TROY SALIBA: The individual animator is not only important, they're everything. The computer is just a tool, and it's only as smart and experienced and intuitive as the person at the other end of the mouse. I keep hearing, "But the computer does it all now." Well, it's not like we type in "awesome photo-real flying monkey that we have an emotional connection to," hit "enter," and the scene unfolds before our eyes. It's still a bunch of talented artists making countless creative decisions on a frame-by-frame basis. And these decisions infiltrate every process: character design and development; the technical aspects of rigging the character; the choices of how the textures look; and setting every key on every frame of animation in order to achieve believable performances. In addition to all of that, the individual artists are critical because there has to be an on-screen cohesiveness between their work and the work of their fellow artists. From animator to animator, shots have the potential to look completely different even though the artists are working with the same model. That's one of the challenges—to make it all feel like there was a singular animator even though dozens of artists put their hands on it.

SCOTT STOKDYK: I agree. There is a team of artists that bring a VFX shot to the place where a CG character can be animated, but from there, most of the life injected into the character is up to the animator. They are guided by Troy, Sam, Bob, others, and myself, but at the end of the day they have to draw from years of experience breathing life into animated creations and make the performance work. We chose not to use motion capture on this project to respect the handmade nature of what we wanted our animation to be. Motion capture is a great tool for a lot of VFX work, but we wanted our Finley and China Girl performances to be brought forth from more than one inspiration. The actor's performance was a primary source, but as you can see, there were many other influences along the way, a big one being the individual animator.

GRANT CURTIS: *We've discussed the importance of the individual, but let's look at another aspect—the technological side. Were there any important groundbreaking techniques and/or technologies created for this film?*

SCOTT STOKDYK: To be sure, there were some incremental improvements in VFX processes employed on this film, but I'd say that the effects in *Oz The Great and Powerful* were executed as more of an artistic labor of love than anything purely technical.

At this point in the evolution of VFX, ground has been broken over and over again to the point that the same ground is being rebroken. At some point, when everything in the frame can be computer generated, it is often more challenging to use real photography even if it will look better. That's where a lot of artistic choices come in, rather than techniques or technologies.

The thing I'm most proud of on this movie is that it has its own unique look and sensibility. It is an interesting combination of retro art design, carefully art-directed sets, and modern VFX execution.

I will say this: if "puppet-cam," or some other form of it has ever been created, I'm unaware of it. I'd consider that groundbreaking.

OZ, walking through a cemetery in the Dark Forest.

GRANT CURTIS: *Can you give us an overview of "puppet-cam" and how it came to be?*

SCOTT STOKDYK: During some of my early conversations with Sam, he challenged us to provide a system that would facilitate capturing the best possible performances from both our on-set actors and our virtual characters. Sam wanted the intimacy and the believability of two actors performing with one another even though one was computer generated.

Traditionally, for movies populated by animated characters, you'll shoot scenes with your actor performing against a tennis ball on a stick. For the most part, you'll get the proper eyelines, but as you can imagine, it has the potential to be a fairly sterile process. Then, several months later, there will be a recording session scheduled and the actor playing the animated character will come in for a couple days and record all of his or her dialogue. The animators will then take the original shot, the recorded dialogue, and animate the virtual character into the scene. Many times, the two actors are never even in the same room together. Sam desperately wanted to avoid such a scenario, thus his challenge.

(THIS PAGE) Zach Braff performs in a scene while in his performance booth as the on-set action plays out before him.

We knew that in order to get Sam what he wanted, we had to have the actors, animated or not, on set or in close proximity. However, we had considerable practical constraints that were not in our favor regardless of how close the computer generated actor could be to set. One of our characters was an eighteen-inch porcelain doll; another was a three-foot-tall flying monkey. Consequently, most of the time these characters were in positions no human could achieve. So, after numerous tests, we created puppet-cam.

Puppet-cam is essentially a real-time videoconference that connects three elements: the actor or actors physically on set, the actor or actors who play animated characters that were in a soundproof booth outside the set, and director Sam Raimi.

For example, let's use a scene in which Oz [James Franco] and Finley [Zach Braff] are walking along the Yellow Brick Road. James was on set wearing an ear wig that allowed him to hear Zach in a recording booth outside, and Zach was getting the production audio feed pumped into him through a set of speakers. At the same time, Sam was wearing a headset that allowed him to speak with both James and Zach. This in itself was complicated, but production sound mixer Petur Hliddal orchestrated it masterfully.

The challenge was how to visually link the three. To achieve this, we manufactured a lightweight monitor that swiveled with a video camera on top of it, and placed that at the end of an adjustable stick manned by a puppeteer. The puppeteer would operate the contraption so that the monitor always faced James and would be where Finley's face would be located if the animated character was real and walking or flying along the Yellow Brick Road. On the monitor was a live feed of Zach from the booth. So, as James was looking at Zach on the monitor, Zach was also seeing James via a feed to a screen in Zach's soundproof booth. For good measure we also put a second monitor in front of Zach that always received the feed from the on-set camera so he would likewise have that reference if he wanted it. Furthermore, while this was going on, Sam was receiving all of these audiovisual feeds on numerous monitors so that he could direct the scene.

Ian Kelley was the video engineer who figured out how to make the whole system work, and it was genius—everyone got what they needed. As mentioned, Zach's booth was soundproof so Petur was able to record his final sound on the spot—we didn't have to come back months later. In addition to the camera that was on Zach's face, we put two other performance capture cameras on each side of him so that we had all the angles covered to capture the nuances of his performance. The animators at Sony Pictures Imageworks were then given the data from these three cameras in order to replicate Zach's performance onto the Finley model—and they got his performances at least six months before they would have received them otherwise. Furthermore, the actors got to act with each other in real-time via a system that naturally created the proper eyelines, and Sam got the organic performances he so desired. It was quite a process to watch in action.

DIRECTOR SAM RAIMI (top left) communicates with the actors on set and in the performance booth with the aid of production sound mixer Petur Hliddal (bottom right). Photographs by Merie Wallace.

GRANT CURTIS: *Similar question in regard to Encodacam. We didn't create it, but it, too, was quite a unique tool. Please give us an Encodacam overview.*

SCOTT STOKDYK: Joe Lewis developed Encodacam in 2003 as a virtual environment visualization tool to help filmmakers with blue-screen or green-screen photography. Basically, it is able to track real camera motion and generate computer renderings of that camera view in real time. The CG environment is composited with the blue screen to give directors and camera operators a preview of what the final composition will look like.

GRANT CURTIS: *In laymen's terms!*

SCOTT STOKDYK: When Sam yells, "Action!" and the camera starts moving, Joe's system adds in an art department-generated background in real time. This combined image is then transmitted to a monitor near Sam so that instead of seeing James walk against a plain blue screen, he sees the proper Oz landscape in the distance that moves and adjusts as the camera does.

JOEY KING in her performance booth and in a fully-realized CG shot from the film. Photograph by Merie Wallace.

GRANT CURTIS: *One more distinctive technological element to describe if you will—the Spheron. What does it do and how does it help the VFX process?*

SCOTT STOKDYK: For the past ten to fifteen years, we've become more and more focused on capturing the director of photography's on-set lighting. We've evolved from shooting chrome spheres that reflect all the lights in the environment, to our latest tool, the Spheron. It's basically a very high-resolution, high-dynamic range camera that, over the course of about a minute and a half, does a 360-degree photographic scan of the environment, including where the lights were placed. Then, when we are back in postproduction adding a CG China Girl into a shot, we know exactly how to light China Girl as Peter Deming would because we have this reference on how he lit the original shot. We can now do in a fraction of the time what used to take five days of artists moving lights around and changing their intensity and direction.

GRANT CURTIS: *Scott touched on this when describing Encodacam, but for this film, practical sets were frequently used in conjunction with computer-generated sets. Why do you think this approach was advantageous creatively? Why not just shoot everything against blue and add it all in via the computer?*

TROY SALIBA: The overall look of the movie benefits because you get a grounded, real-world sense of lighting and texture that the effects artists are able to use as reference for their extensions. As far as the actors are concerned, anytime you have more of the tangible world around them, it's always going to affect their performance positively—it's going to help them get into the moment. There are very few scenarios on this film where the actors are standing in a solitary field of blue, having to imagine the world around them while delivering a performance. They can focus more on the emotional intent of the scene they're in rather than imagining the environment they are standing on. There have been movies in the past where you can actually sense that the actors felt a little out of place when they are in a predominantly blue-screen environment. This film benefits from having at least the immediate world that's around the actors.

SCOTT STOKDYK: I agree, and it's interesting because the ramifications of building a practical set, versus putting up a blue screen and then adding the world digitally, are far more complex and impactful than most people realize. Think about it this way—when filming on a practical set, the art directors and the cinematographer work together to create a shot that looks appropriate for the scene and story. With a few exceptions, there is an advantage to choosing this route because everything you shoot will, in theory, automatically look real—it's actually there. When you elect to use a blue screen and create the environment using computer graphics, you have the same goal as when shooting on a practical set, but with the added challenge of needing to make the environment look real. If you are creating something in the computer that could have been built practically and lit, the best you can hope for is that it will look as good as if it was actually created and shot on set. At worst, it will not be believable or it will not give the desired look and feel of the environment.

(THESE PAGES) A before and after example of how a combination of practical sets and CG wizardry achieved the look of the Land of Oz, while at the same time giving the actors tangible real estate with which to interact. Photograph by Merie Wallace.

The flip side of this is that many settings are cost prohibitive, impossible to shoot, or simply don't exist in the natural world. In these instances, the only option is to embrace computer graphics. This was often the case on *Oz The Great and Powerful* because we have a fantastical world that does not exist in nature. Therefore, by design, we were restricted to soundstages, and anything with large outdoor scope had to be shot against blue screen and then added in digitally. In those cases, we worked with the art department and almost always had a critical portion of the set or landscape—no matter how small—in the frame. Those tangible assets then formed the base from which we built, lit, and textured the CG surroundings, and as a result we got the best of both worlds: the photo-realism of a tangible set or environment blended with a fantastical world.

This realism would not have been possible without the collaboration between VFX and the art department. Even though there is a team of hundreds of digital artists in postproduction, not all of them have the specialized set-design and decoration skills that on-set crews have. Therefore, it is immensely important for the decision-makers in the postproduction VFX process to incorporate the talents of the film's art department. When we started *Oz The Great and Powerful*, our VFX goal for CG environments was to make them feel like an extension of our real sets, while giving them scope, and we've achieved that.

JAMES FRANCO views a scene with the blue-screen background, and, with the aid of Encodacam, views the scene with the Oz landscape added in. Photograph by Merie Wallace.

JAMES FRANCO has a conversation with his CG sidekick, China Girl, in this final frame from the film.

GRANT CURTIS: *It takes over two years to make a project like* Oz The Great and Powerful. *That is a lifetime in the digital world. How are you able to stay ahead of the curve so that by the time the film comes out it does not look dated?*

SCOTT STOKDYK: On *Oz The Great and Powerful*, we have one distinct advantage in that its look and feel has a classic, timeless sensibility. We are not chasing flashy, modern, or trendy results. Instead, we are crafting a look rooted in a very traditional Hollywood aesthetic. I hope the audience appreciates *Oz The Great and Powerful* as a great fantasy story with heart, but I also hope they appreciate the handcrafted feel. We're trying to bring a heart and soul to the visuals that are grounded in reality. We're not just using technology for the technology's sake, but trying to use the right tool for the desired result.

To that end, any time a VFX concept would come up that would seem like a "modern" effect, I would constantly be examining it and rethinking the process. As an example, we would try to do some of the witch transformations off camera and reveal them with edits, rather than doing in-camera morphs. Also, our VFX directive for the witch's magic was to mimic how a practical-effects person would do it on set, then enhance that version. As a result of this directive, I think this film is going to stand the test of time to a greater degree than most.

GRANT CURTIS: *Scott, you mention this directive, which came from Sam. He plays a massive part in the VFX process on all his films. This is your fourth film with him—what do you feel he brings to the table, and how has Sam changed throughout the years?*

SCOTT STOKDYK: First and foremost, Sam is such a visual director. He's known as a great actor's director, and he works extremely well with actors, but what I love is that he's able to get the drama and the performance you care about with a great visual style.

ZACH BRAFF, SAM RAIMI, AND JAMES FRANCO (opposite page) watch as China Girl prepares for her close-up (this page). Photographs by Merie Wallace.

Sam's also inventive. When I first started working with him on *Spider-Man*, he came from a pre-digital world of effects. He didn't have much digital experience at that point. In the early days, I think he was a little more tentative, but by now he knows the tools, knows their limits, and knows how to push them. He loves to use existing tools and old-school tricks, as well as new technologies, to create interesting shots. It's this inventiveness that keeps it interesting. Working with Sam over the years I've learned to expect the unexpected. I know that on the day Sam's going to come up with new ideas that challenge and push us. I can't just prepare for what I know is coming, I have to prepare for all the challenges lurking in that brain of his.

What's been unique to *Oz The Great and Powerful* is watching his transition from 2-D to 3-D—and it's been a very natural one. That's not surprising considering he's always used depth in a 3-D fashion. He's always been concerned compositionally with things coming toward and away from the audience. The classic limits of 3-D and the "gotchas" haven't been an issue because his head already works in that space.

(THESE PAGES) James Franco enacts the action within a scene in which Oscar Diggs flies over the Land of Oz via bubble. Photographs by Merie Wallace.

GRANT CURTIS: *Looking back, how has* Oz The Great and Powerful *been a unique experience for you?*

SCOTT STOKDYK: It's been unique in that our overall approach has resulted in a fascinating application of VFX. *Oz The Great and Powerful* would not have been made the same way twenty years ago, and probably would not be done in the same way if it had happened twenty years in the future. We are at a great crossroads where we can combine live-action and CG in interesting ways, when the trend in the economics of filmmaking seems to point to a future where most things will be too costly to do practically, and have to be done in CG. I feel lucky to have worked on a show where you can still combine the best of live-action and CG into the VFX process.

(THIS PAGE) Director Sam Raimi discusses Oscar's flight with James Franco. Photograph by Merie Wallace.

(OPPOSITE PAGE) A before and after study of this voyage.

TROY SALIBA: I don't know if it was because
it was shot on location in Michigan for five
months, or because it was all on a soundstage,
but the time on set, more than any of my other
experiences, feels like it influenced the mood of
the entire movie. It's hard to explain, but there
was an intangible that was heightened on this
movie. I'm sure it was a combination of working
with Sam, the sets, the actors, the costumes,
and the people that created this energy that has
floated through the production. The experience
was magical and really informed this sense of
fantasy that the movie has. When I can, I try to
instill that in the artists I work with in the hope
that somehow a little sense of that electricity will
make it into the animated performances.

PHOTOGRAPH BY
Merie Wallace.

CHAPTER VI

LIVING
IN THE LAND OF OZ
THE GREAT AND POWERFUL

MEETING THE ACTORS

ROLL B13   SCENE 6U   TAKE 1

B 1:10 72 924   7/29

The
OZ GREAT and POWERFUL

Dir: S. Raimi
Cam: P. Deming ASC

PHOTOGRAPH BY
Merie Wallace.

JAMES FRANCO

Oz

"When you work with James, you're not just working with an actor, you're working with a fellow filmmaker. It's like two comrades making a film together."

SAM RAIMI, *director*

For actor James Franco, the occasion to play the titular character in *Oz The Great and Powerful* meant the chance to portray one of the first literary characters he ever met on the page. As a young child, Franco's first narrative experience was reading all fourteen of L. Frank Baum's Oz books, and he was excited by the prospect of transporting one of the characters of his youth to the silver screen. "I thought the role provided an opportunity to create something that linked to a classic character, but also provided room for a fresh take" comments Franco.

There was indeed space for Franco to leave his mark on the beloved character of Oscar Zoroaster Phadrig Isaac Norman Henkle Emmanuel Ambroise Diggs, aka Oz. (Baum devotees will recall Oz's initials spell OZ PINHEAD.) In the Baum books, the Wizard is an old humbug, which begs the question: "What was Oz like as a young man?" The filmmakers wrestled with this question as they mapped out *Oz The Great and Powerful*, ultimately crafting the character as a young man with a bevy of flaws. "The film is about a man who is a magician in a traveling circus," Franco says. "Oz is a bit of a con man, and a bit of a Lothario. He's a selfish guy, and then he gets whisked off to this fantastical world where he is confronted with all of his issues."

Peeling back the layers of James' character to explore these issues was a friend and ally, director Sam Raimi. "This is our fourth film together," Franco says, referring to their work on the three Spider-Man films, "and not only is Sam an incredibly fun director to work with, but he's brilliant on the technical side of things; the way he composes a movie, the pacing and the editing. Sam has always been a very collaborative director. He looks to his actors and the people around him for contributions and he's very open to other people's ideas."

(OPPOSITE PAGE) Sam Raimi and James Franco discuss one of the first shots filmed for *Oz The Great and Powerful*, and shake hands after James' final shot. Photographs by Merie Wallace.

(TOP) Oz discusses the intricacies of black powder with some of the Munchkins. Photograph by Merie Wallace.

(BOTTOM RIGHT) Oz as the humbug from Baum's books and as originally sketched by W.W. Denslow.

In an effort to fully embody Oz, Franco was also called upon to tap into his magical side. While the three witches do in fact have true magical powers, Oz relies on sleight of hand and misdirection to give the illusion of magic. In order to convincingly portray Oz as a carnival-show magician, Franco had to partake in several weeks of training. "I was asked to come out two weeks in advance so that I could work with the great Lance Burton, one of the most famous, if not the most famous magician, from Las Vegas," Franco explains. "We worked together every day on certain magic tricks. Producing doves out of nothing, and creating fire out of my hand and turning that into a dove. I got them down pretty well."

For Franco, these experiences added to a character that was already multilayered and made Oz all the more relatable. "The character was written in a certain way—part con man, part seducer, part vaudeville guy, all of which appealed to me," elaborates Franco. "In some ways, he touches on many aspects of Americana, while being a cross between Charlie Chaplin and Clark Gable. He is a goofball, and a dashing kind of guy, but a guy maybe not equipped in the traditional ways of being a hero. He has unconventional ways of tackling his problems and fumbling through them. I love the character because of all that."

On *Oz The Great and Powerful,* Franco got the opportunity to work with a director he admires while paying homage to a character he met on the page years ago. And, for director Sam Raimi, James has the perfect qualities to bring the iconic Wizard from Baum's adventures to audiences worldwide. "For this role, I don't think it would have worked as well with an actor who is selfish inside. We needed somebody who is in touch with his emotions because he plays a character with a good heart. I really needed an actor who had that quality within him. James, while funny and loving, has got real heart that he shares with the audience."

MILA KUNIS

THEODORA/WICKED WITCH OF THE WEST

"I've worked with Mila in numerous things, and I can say that she is one of my favorite actresses to work with, ever. She is easygoing, smart, has great instincts, and I think we have good chemistry."

JAMES FRANCO, actor (Oz)

Transformation is at the heart of Mila Kunis' role in *Oz The Great and Powerful*. She plays Theodora, the young, naive, lovestruck girl who becomes, through manipulation and heartbreak, the infamous Wicked Witch of the West. For Kunis, it was not just a transformation for the character, but for her as an actress as well. "What intrigued me about this was the unknown. I've never done anything remotely close to this," comments Kunis. "No one has ever trusted me with anything like this, but you have to challenge yourself, and I felt safe in the challenge because I was surrounded by people that I respect so much—Sam first and foremost."

In order to maker her more comfortable with taking on such an iconic role, director Sam Raimi met with Kunis to discuss the story and the role of Theodora. "What was supposed to be a thirty-minute meeting ended up being four hours long," she says. "We ended up breaking down the character and the script and grounding everything in reality, which was incredibly comforting to me." By meeting's end, Kunis was ready to become the Wicked Witch.

Part of Kunis' initial hesitation stems from the profound respect she has for the Land of Oz. Kunis, who is originally from the Ukraine, moved to the United States when she was seven years old. "I loved *The Wonderful Wizard of Oz* when I was little. It was so magical and beautiful," she says. "My brother used to read the Russian version, and I always thought it was a Russian book until I came to America. When we moved, my parents were trying to get me to read in English and they figured, why not give her something she likes.

MILA GETS A MAKEUP touch-up by Howard Berger in full Wicked Witch gear (this page); as the naive and lovely Theodora, with Oz (oppose page). Photographs by Merie Wallace.

While the Wicked Witch of the West may be one of the world's most iconic characters, very little is told of how she came to be the terror of Oz. As we come to find out, the gnarled old witch was once just an innocent girl who suffered a broken heart. "When we first meet her, she is very demure and very sweet," Kunis explains, but then she meets the Wizard. "It's her first crush. Imagine being fifteen and thinking you've found the love of your life. Every girl is going to identify with Theodora. She's a girl who desperately wants to believe in good, and believe in the better of society, the better of people, and the better of the world. And she falls in love, gets her heart broken, and can't deal with it. Everybody goes through a moment where they wish they didn't have to feel pain."

Birthed from that pain is one of the greatest villains ever seen, and as Kunis comes to the end of her most recent transformation, she is looking forward to seeing how audiences react. "I hope they smile," she says. "I hope they enjoy themselves. If they have a great time, that's all I can hope for."

RACHEL WEISZ

EVANORA/WICKED WITCH OF THE EAST

"Rachel's portrayal of the calculating and evil Evanora is addictive. You can't look away—you're drawn to her. As an actress, she's one of the best of her generation. As an actress playing the embodiment of pure, manipulative evil, she's peerless."

GRANT CURTIS, *executive producer*

From *The Mummy* to *About a Boy* to *The Constant Gardener*—a movie that led to an Academy Award, a Golden Globe, and a Screen Actors Guild Award for Best Actress—Rachel Weisz has excelled in everything from high drama to romantic comedy. Yet despite her varied and impressive resume, there was still something about Evanora, one of the Wicked Witches of *Oz The Great and the Powerful*, that compelled the talented actress to take on the role of the Wicked Witch of the East. "She's rotten to the core—manipulative, cruel, evil. Evanora has a lot of fun being bad," Weisz says of her character, "and I think that is what appealed to me."

For Weisz, the role also presented an opportunity to bring life to a character that, for over a century, had before only been seen as a pair of feet. However, in *Oz The Great and Powerful*, audiences will get to see her head to toe, and at the height of her power. "I'm a very manipulative dictator who's spinning a lot of evil stories to tell the people of Oz," explains Weisz.

Director Sam Raimi could not have been more pleased with Weisz's portrayal. "I love Rachel's performance as Evanora. She's got to make you believe she is the advisor to the king and a good person—someone who's just looking out for the welfare of the Emerald City and its inhabitants," elaborates Raimi. "Later, when we realize that she's the Wicked Witch, we finally can see the darkness that runs through her. She's as wicked as they come."

As a result, when Weisz found out that she was up for the role of a wicked witch, she didn't hesitate, and Raimi's participation only made the role that much more enticing. "The chance to work with Sam was very exciting," Weisz says. "I think he brings an incredible passion and an amazing childlike imagination to this project. He has this beautiful ability to tell stories that have an innocence and clarity that children can relate to and that adults find engaging. He's a really wonderful storyteller. I've enjoyed being directed by him."

In addition to her collaboration with Sam, acting across from the likes of James Franco, Mila Kunis, and Michelle Williams was also an enjoyable experience for Weisz. "James is very comedic, very funny. He brings levity, and a lot of charm," she says of her scenes with Oz. "And it's been great working with Michelle Williams. She exemplifies pure good, and I'm pure evil, and it's been really fun being her enemy. We get along very well off-set, so I'm allowed to be incredibly mean to her when the camera is rolling," Weisz declares with a smile. "It's fun. She's a really incredible actress." Rachel also had fun with her "younger sister." "Mila has got really great range," Weisz observes. "She makes this incredible transformation into being wicked and evil, and Mila has really embraced it."

With an all-star cast, an admired director, and an enticing role, the chance to work on *Oz The Great and Powerful* was an opportunity not lost on Weisz. "This was a great project to be asked to join," she says. Luckily for fans, Weisz pushed any concerns aside and created a truly memorable villain, from what had been merely a pair of striped stockings and famous slippers.

RACHEL WEISZ rehearses a stunt for the film (opposite page), and she discusses a scene with director Sam Raimi (this page). Photographs by Merie Wallace.

MICHELLE WILLIAMS

ANNIE / GLINDA THE GOOD WITCH OF THE SOUTH

"*Michelle has a real depth of spirit and soul. She's a very good person and I needed that in the actress who was going to play Glinda, because when the camera gets really close and you look into an actor's eyes, you can see if they've got a good soul or not.*"

SAM RAIMI, director

For Michelle Williams, who breathes new life into an icon in *Oz The Great and Powerful*, the role of Glinda meant a lot of responsibility. Yet, it was a role she was eager to tackle. "I was really excited to play Glinda," Williams says. "She is the embodiment of everything that is honest, unselfish, and pure."

Like other actors in the film who play dual characters, Williams has a role in both the "real" world and in the Land of Oz. In Kansas, Williams is Annie, Oz's frustrated love interest. They have known each other since they were children, and while Annie tries to get Oz to commit and embrace his inner good, her efforts are in vain. In *Oz The Great and Powerful*, Williams portrays Glinda the Good Witch of the South, who has more luck. "Annie and Glinda always believe the best in Oz, and that view is rewarded at the end of the movie when he grows into the man they always knew he was," comments Williams. "He was the only one who couldn't see it."

At the onset of this awakening for Oz, when the audience first meets Glinda, she is shrouded in darkness and unrecognizable. She reveals herself to Oscar as the Good Witch of the South and explains that she has been waiting for him. "There is a prophecy that a great wizard is going to fall from the sky and deliver Oz from the tyranny of the evil witches," Williams explains. "And so Glinda meets Oz and has really high hopes for who he is and what he is going to do for her people—and then she has to come to terms with the fact that he is not quite what she expected." Luckily for Oz, Glinda has a knack for bringing out the best in people, and her belief in him helps him to grow and learn to believe in himself. Their relationship is, in many ways, the backbone of the film, supporting the story and keeping everyone together.

Glinda's kindness and virtue was also reflected in her wardrobe. Michelle and costume designer Gary Jones spent countless hours making sure her wardrobe reflected the traditional look of a princess with the strength of a leader and the magic of a witch. Unlike the other witches whose wardrobes darken in tone as they grow more evil, it was important that Glinda's costume colors retained the same hues throughout the film, which were a reflection of her goodness and purity. "Her first dress and her warrior dress are all translucent and opaque," Jones explains. "They are all shades of white and opalescent."

Even when Glinda must partake in battle, her dress remains a reflection of her character as she remains a beacon of light, guiding her people and giving hope to everyone. "I like that when we meet her," Williams says of her character, "she's more demure and cloaked in these very delicate fabrics. Then, as the battle dawns, she suits up in something that is slightly tougher and more like armor. It's like fairy-princess armor, but it's armor nevertheless." On-screen, Williams glows in her outfits, something that was not surprising to Jones. "Michelle brings a wonderful sense of what it is to be good and benevolent. She's a joy in every way."

Williams herself found the project "to be a dream on a couple levels. For me, to go to work every day with Sam and this cast and to exist in the space of Glinda the Good Witch of the South has been amazing. I didn't know that work could be this much fun. I think I had lost sight of that somewhere along the way and I was excited every day to be there.

"Being able to work with people who are really at the top of their games was so exciting," continues Williams with praise for both the film's artistry and the experience itself. "The sets and the costumes were beyond my expectations. I couldn't imagine things that big and that beautiful, and I got to play inside that world every day."

(OPPOSITE PAGE) Michelle Williams poses with her magical wand (bottom left), and Michelle Williams and James Franco take in the sights before them (top right). Photographs by Merie Wallace.

(THIS PAGE) Michelle Williams dives into a pile of foam blocks for a stunt she performed (bottom left), and she takes a break with Zach Braff (top right). Photographs by Merie Wallace.

ZACH BRAFF

FRANK/FINLEY

"Working with Zach was easy from the beginning. We got along incredibly well. There needed to be a dynamic between Oz and Finley that was antagonistic but very funny. I see it as akin to Laurel and Hardy. I felt like Zach was the perfect person to develop that relationship with."

JAMES FRANCO, *actor (Oz)*

Known for his roles in *Scrubs* and independent films such as *Garden State*, actor/writer/director/producer Zach Braff decided he wanted to "take on something different." When offered the role of Finley the flying monkey in *Oz The Great and Powerful*, different is exactly what he got. "Everything about it interested me," says Braff. "If you look at the scale of this movie, it's epic. I'd never been a part of a gargantuan studio tentpole movie before, so that was exciting for me."

In the film, Zach plays dual roles. "Some of the characters that exist within the world of Kansas are transplanted to the world of Oz," he explains. During the opening scenes in the Sunflower State, Braff plays Frank, Oz's put-upon and beleaguered assistant. He is tasked with pulling people in to see Oz's show and, far too often, protecting the magician from his various indiscretions. "He walks all over me," Braff says, "and I do all his bidding, and he has no interest in being my friend."

When the tornado sweeps Oz up and away, Frank is left behind...in a sense. Once in the Land of Oz, Braff reappears as the voice of Finley, a flying, talking monkey, recently displaced from his home due to an attack from the Wicked Witch. "This is a hybrid character," Braff says, "part human, with mostly human characteristics, but a flying monkey."

In the initial script, Finley was written as a supporting character, providing a few laughs while accompanying Oz down the Yellow Brick Road. When the cameras started rolling, however, it became clear to filmmakers that the role of Finley needed to be expanded. Braff's humor and his chemistry with the other actors made for great scenes. Taking note of that, changes were made to the script. In the final film, Finley and Oz become pals almost immediately, something that allowed the character to be developed into something much more significant. "Finley is the Wizard's conscience," director Raimi explains. "When he gets to Oz, Finley reminds the Wizard in so many different ways about right and wrong. At first, Oz doesn't listen, but eventually he begins to respect the monkey. His most important affect on Oz is that of a good friend who reminds you that you're not living up to your expectations, and that you have to do a lot better."

For Zach, who studied film at Northwestern University, being part of *Oz The Great and Powerful* not only gave him the chance to experience filmmaking at such a large scale, but it also gave him the opportunity to work with a director he had always respected. "I've always looked up to Sam, whose work I really admire," Braff says. "He's just so friendly, and genuinely interested in what his actors think. He's collaborative. Not only is he a tremendous filmmaker, but he's just a wonderful person."

With a supportive director and all-star cast, Braff's first role in a major tentpole movie has been a magical experience, and he is certain they've done it right.

(OPPOSITE PAGE) Zach Braff mans the Finley stand-in while in a scene with James Franco. Photograph by Merie Wallace.

(THIS PAGE) Actor Zach Braff jokes around on set. Photograph by Merie Wallace.

JOEY KING

WHEELCHAIR GIRL/CHINA GIRL

"Joey's amazing. She's an old soul—so smart and articulate. When I first met her, she was giving her thoughts on a scene to Sam and he was listening to her so intently. Little by little she starts to make the most amazing, deep, intuitive, and intellectual point. She's a great kid and a really good actress."

ZACH BRAFF, actor (Frank/Finley)

Joey King was born ninety-nine years after the first L. Frank Baum book was published. Yet, in spite of this age gap, the world of Oz still resonates with the young actress. "When I first saw the movie, I loved everything about it. I was just happy," proclaims King.

Although a town made of china was in Baum's first novel, this is the first time her character will appear in print or on the big screen—and King could not be more excited to make China Girl a new favorite for audiences. For Joey, whose first lead role came in 2010 when she played Ramona in *Ramona and Beezus*, China Girl is a big step. While she has plenty of credits to her name—ranging from appearances on television in *CSI*, *Entourage*, and *Ghost Whisperer*, and films such as *Quarantine*; *Battle: Los Angeles*; *Crazy, Stupid, Love*; *Reign Over Me*; and *The Dark Knight Rises*—this role is arguably her biggest to date.

Like Zach Braff, who has dual roles in the film, King also tackles two characters. In Kansas, she plays a girl who requests Oz's help but is rebuffed. However, the majority of King's role begins when she reappears in the world of Oz as China Girl and becomes, in many ways, Oz's moral compass. Throughout the rest of the film, when Oscar tries to veer off his path or take the coward's way out, China Girl, with her angelic face and pure heart, is among those who reel him back in.

As is the case with Finley the flying monkey, China Girl is a CG character, which made filming a unique experience for King. In order to make sure the character seemed as real as possible, the filmmakers brought in the talented puppeteer Phillip Huber, who created a life-size marionette of the China Girl that he manipulated as King provided the voice. "They didn't do motion capture with me," King explains. "When I arrived on set for rehearsals, Sam would say 'Joey, how would you do that? Would you put this hand out, or this one, or would you put both hands on your hips?' I would do the motions while they were doing the scene." Those motions would be mimicked by Huber via the puppet and then later manipulated in the CG process to bring the China Girl to life.

When seen on the big screen, the China Girl will not only have King's voice and mimic her movements, but her facial expressions too. King was filmed by the VFX team as she read her lines, and those images were later used to animate the China Girl's face. "It's like nothing I've ever done before," she says. Luckily for King, she had a supportive director in Sam Raimi. "He's really precise and picks up on the little details," King says about Raimi. "It makes all the difference. It's amazing the way he works."

Not only did the movie allow her the chance to collaborate with Raimi, it also gave King the chance to work with a group of actors whom she admires greatly. In many ways, the feeling on set mimicked the feeling at the end of the movie—everyone became a family. "James and Zach like to tease me," she says, laughing. "They're like big brothers. And Michelle is so sweet. She is like a motherly figure, and Mila is an older sister."

By the end of *Oz The Great and Powerful*, the China Girl has found a new home in the Emerald City, a new father figure in Oz, and a new sense of peace. "She has people to trust and she has people who will be there for her," King states. In a sense, making this film echoed that sentiment for Joey King. The movie gave her a new cast of friends and unforgettable memories of her own.

"I hope the audience will laugh and fall in love with the Wizard as he falls in love. I hope they are terrorized by the Wicked Witch and the baboons. I think there are some surprises waiting for them down the Yellow Brick Road."

SAM RAIMI, *director*